# EASY WAYS
## WITH

# *DRIED*
# *FLOWERS*

# EASY WAYS
## WITH

# *DRIED*
# *FLOWERS*

### AMELIA
### SAINT GEORGE

SMITHMARK

*To Alex*

First published in Great Britain in 1992 by Anaya Publishers Ltd
Strode House, 44–50 Osnaburgh Street, London NW1 3ND
Reprinted 1993

This edition published in 1994 by SMITHMARK Publishers Inc.,
16 East 32nd Street, New York, NY 10016.

SMITHMARK books are available for bulk purchase for sales
promotion and premium use. For details write or call the
manager of special sales, SMITHMARK Publishers Inc., 16
East 32nd Street, New York, NY 10016; (212) 532-6600.

Produced by Anaya Publishers Ltd., 3rd Floor, Strode House,
44–50 Osnaburgh Street, London NW1 3ND.

ISBN 0–8317–3783–2

Printed in Hong Kong

10 9 8 7 6 5 4 3 2 1

# Contents

# Introduction

The wonderful variety of colors, tones, textures, and shapes that dried flowers offer is truly inspirational. Yet the most exciting displays can be created using the simplest of techniques.

In this book, I have endeavored to reveal some of the mysteries of dried flower style and inspire those interested in this pastime to attempt really ambitious projects and achieve the most spectacular results with ease.

Dried flowers are extraordinarily flexible, with few of the constraints of their fresh counterparts. For this reason, they can be treated in a completely different way. You can hang them upside down, weave them in your hair, or tie them around presents.

Each display in this book, grand or humble, is beautifully photographed and clearly explained. Where necessary, illustrations are provided to help you understand a more intricate technique.

However, my approach is often a little unorthodox, and I encourage cheating where possible! Glue and tape are great allies and make assembling materials considerably easier.

I have also encouraged gathering your own materials for preservation. Country walks, visits to the beach, windfallen treasures from city parks, or even your own yard can be a rich source. Wherever you live, there is always some treat to be gathered and saved for later.

It is also challenging and fun to experiment. Do not be restricted to traditional materials. I have used eggs, fungi, nuts, bread, beads, natural burrs and vines, herbs and spices as well as more popular ingredients. You can add to the list: shells, stones, driftwood, seeds, and berries, just for example.

I have also explained various techniques for drying and preserving flowers based upon my own experience and mistakes! Do not be daunted by the prospect that this is a highly scientific process; often, the simplest way to dry most flowers is to tie them in bunches and hang them upside down in your attic!

I hope this book will stimulate your imagination and act as an inspirational tool. I also hope you will be encouraged to copy, adapt, or move on further and create your own unique displays.

# PLANTING
# IN
# ROWS

One wonderful advantage of dried
floral material is its ability to
become virtually an abstract art
form in its own right, allowing
those with a keen eye to exploit this
for visual excitement.

In this chapter, I have looked at
using the sharper angles of various
floral materials: the upright stems,
the acute edges of cut spices and
herbs, or even the straight lines of
the container, and exploiting them
to the full. All use rows of similarly
sized materials, planted in military
precision.

I have created both the avant-garde
and the more traditional using this
technique. I think you will agree
that the effects of these displays is
stunning; yet the skills to create
them is minimal. Use the ideas on
the following pages to inspire you to
try others.

# Rose baskets

The radiant beauty and vibrant colors of the rose in the fullness of its life give way to more subtle tones and textures when it is dried. Compact buds and blooms; fat, burgeoning rose hips; fragrant petals evoking the bouquet of summer days for winter nights – at every stage in its development, the delightful rose is a perfect choice for preservation.

Dried roses are easy to arrange, providing the display is well-structured, and planting in rows or clusters is an ideal starting point.

With these three rose designs, the Lavender Basket and the Herb and Spice garden later in this chapter, you will be able to combine orderly precision with charm and style.

### TALL STANDING ROSES

Gather together 60–80 beautiful roses – I have used 'Gerdo' – and a plain round basket for the simplest of all arrangements. Have at hand florist foam, thread, and sharp scissors. Wide gauzy, chiffon ribbon in two pastel shades will complete the display.

Begin by cutting a piece of florist foam to fit snugly inside your basket. Sort your roses into two piles: one with straight stems and the other with curved stems. Strip off any damaged leaves.

To retain a flat, tailored look to the roses, elevate your arrangement to eye level. When possible, I sit while arranging, so put my basket on several large books or telephone directories.

Take one curved-stemmed rose and plant it into the center of the foam. This will govern the height of your arrangement, so check that none of your remaining roses is too short. You may need to trim the original.

Each rose will need to stand at the same height, so you may need to trim some stems as you work.

Place the next rose against the first, always applying pressure to the base of the stem when inserting it into the foam. (Never push from the bud end or the stem might snap.)

Continue using your curved-stemmed roses, planting evenly from the center out. Strip off undamaged leaves as you go, so the arrangement does not become too bulky. These pieces of foliage can be used later to fill in any gaps.

Having used all your curved-stemmed roses, continue working out to the edge of the basket using the straight-stemmed flowers. The straight stems will conceal the curved ones. Tuck a few pieces of foliage upright in any empty-looking spots and tie a piece of thread around the stems to mark the position of the ribbon. Cut a generous length of ribbon and tie it in a relaxed, floppy bow to cover the thread.

*Tall and elegant, these salmon-colored rose heads sit proudly aloft their dense green leaves in a natural twig basket. Placing them in rows like this creates interesting straight lines and sharp angles not usually associated with flowers. Here, the straight stems are echoed by the vertical lines of the basket. The whole effect is softened by gauze ribbon which also complements the lovely colors of the blooms.*

## ROSE HEARTS

Once again, I allowed the design of my container to guide me. This charming heart-shaped basket, woven from vines, lent itself perfectly to this technique of planting in rows.

Florist foam, roses, and sharp scissors were all that I needed to gather together before I began. I used the rich scarlet 'Mercedes' variety of rose.

I packed each heart-shape with florist foam and began planting my roses, using curved-stemmed roses in the center of the middle heart, working outward and finishing toward the rim with the straighter stems, in exactly the same way that I planted the larger display.

Work the outside heart-shapes, once the middle one is complete.

Do remember always to push your rose into the foam from the base of the stem, to avoid any possibility of breaking it.

Keep the roses close together so that the heads look tightly packed. It does mean that even for small baskets such as this, you will still need a lot of blooms for the design to work well and create a sense of density.

To add interest to this display and to exploit the lovely container, I placed the sections at three different heights. For the right-hand heart, I trimmed the roses to sit into the basket, with just their heads peeping over the rim; for the left-hand heart, the roses stand tall and proud.

Although you may not be able to find a container exactly like this one, there are many similar designs available, often very inexpensive to purchase.

*Adapt the technique of planting in rows to any container. This unusual triple heart basket worked well when planted in tiers with scarlet roses. The dense, dark green foliage is vital to achieve a good effect. Fill in any gaps with scraps of foliage you have already stripped off other stems.*

## PETAL PALISADE

The vertical lines of this elegant wire basket create a perfect setting for these 'Ilseta' roses. I have used about 180 flower heads; obviously, you can achieve the same effect with a smaller basket and fewer blooms. The basket is filled to the brim with fragrant rose petals and lavender.

To begin, gather together the roses, petals, and loose lavender. These last two items can either be bought ready-prepared, as potpourri, or you can collect your own from damaged blooms and stems. You will also need a wire basket, a glue gun, and some plain lining paper.

Line the base of the basket with paper, then start to insert the roses into the slats of the wire basket. Work the corners first – from bottom to top – pushing the roses into the slats, one at a time, overlapping the stems within the basket as shown. Glue each rose lightly to the wire and to the rose beneath.

Continue working the sides in the same way, but do not overlap the stems.

Once the basket is lined with glorious blooms, fill to the brim with rose petals and lavender heads. For economy, fill the basket with natural fiber (available from nurseries) first before topping it up with petals and flower heads.

*Hearts and roses are synonymous, so this lovely wire basket made in the shape of a heart was a perfect foil for these pretty pink 'Ilseta' roses. As the roses lie horizontally, this design is an interesting variation on planting in rows. The Petal Palisade uses flowers only to decorate the perimeter of the basket; inside it is filled with potpourri made from rose petals and lavender.*

*To create a tight angle on a basket such as this, you will need to overlap each stem as you insert the roses. Dab a spot of glue on the basket and the rose beneath.*

# Lavender basket

*Lavender is one of the most popular flowers used for planting in rows. Upright stems and small flowerheads gain strength and substance when clustered together like this. Once again, the lines of the stems follow those of the basket beneath. A complementary bow in bright lavender-purple completes the display.*

Aromatic, delicate, and whimsical, this display captures the image of lavender fields in Provençe rippling in the wind like purple waves.

You will need a profusion of lavender for this design, but remember it is simple to dry it yourself if you are fortunate enough to be able to gather it locally.

A simple basket, florist foam, scissors, and a coordinating ribbon are the only other materials you will need.

Tightly pack your chosen basket full of florist foam. As the lavender will stand right at the basket's edge, make sure the foam fills the basket completely.

As with the roses, sort your lavender into curved stems and straight stems, forming two piles. Cut the lavender stems to the same length using sharp scissors.

As lavender is delicate, there will be damaged flower heads; do not use them in the arrangement as they will spoil it. Instead, save them for potpourri.

Now begin planting the lavender, using the curved stems first in the center of the display, rather as you did for the tall standing roses. Work with the flower heads at eye level so you can keep the display as flat as possible.

Use up the curved stems in the center of the arrangement, progressing to the straighter stems for the outer edges. Place them right up to the basket's edge.

Once complete, place a purple ribbon gently around the display. A final little trick: spray the display with some firm-hold hairspray: the lavender will shed less and last longer.

## POTPOURRI
Save damaged lavender to make potpourri. Rub the flowerheads gently in your finger to remove them from their stems. This action will also release the lavender's distinctive aroma.

# Herb and spice garden

Musky cinnamon, warm nutmeg, spicy chili peppers, and mellow bay leaves lay side by side in neat rows divided by startling fungal shapes. This is a stunning and eye-catching arrangement, perfect for kitchen displays or those to accompany haute cuisine; and the sweet and sharp aromas make it an interesting alternative to potpourri.

A wide, flat container is needed here, along with a flat piece of florist foam, sharp scissors, and knife, and glue to secure some of the pieces.

Line your container with foam, then experiment, forming one row of the various ingredients, placing them along the foam to judge the best positioning.

For my container, I began with the center row of golden mushroom and worked outward using cinnamon, nutmeg, and chili in that order, with bay leaves along the outer edge. When you are happy with the position of one row, you can begin the arrangement in earnest.

Begin with the center row – the mushrooms – starting from the back of the basket and working forward. Overlap each piece of fungus very slightly and glue each one in place, as you work. Progress forward, allowing the last piece of fungus to lap gently over the front edge of the basket to finish that row neatly.

Next, using the depth of your basket as a guide, cut the cinnamon sticks with sharp scissors, taking care they do not crumble. Push each piece upright into the foam on each side of the fungus.

Next to the cinnamon, glue the whole nutmegs into position.

Now sort the bay leaves, disregarding those that are too large or small. Cut each one carefully in half across the width, so they do not crack. Slip the leaves, pointed ends down, snugly against one another, working from the back of the basket to the front, to create miniature clipped hedges.

Finally, cut the chilis to fill in the gaps between the bay and the nutmeg. Some may need to be glued into place.

*Another interesting variation on planting in rows, this Herb and Spice Garden is a great conversation piece with its abstract shapes and angular lines. Display it on a low windowseat or ledge where it can be viewed from above to give it maximum impact. Almost any plants or seeds can be planted in this way, with contrasting shapes and textures lying side by side.*

Plan your herb and spice garden by experimenting with one row of items first. From this, you can judge the balance of color, shape, and texture.

# TOPIARY TREES

*The formal structures of the trees in this chapter make enduring and eye-catching arrangements. The more familiar trees with a trunk and flower-filled top are here, but I have also demonstrated some cunning variations using teasels and eggs.*

*The principle is to keep the ingredients to a minimum; use only one or two varieties for the main element and perhaps just one for filling out the sphere.*

*I have explained how to create the more traditional tree, but I have also used a basic foam cone to make another tree shape. The latter concept could easily be adapted for Christmas decorations.*

# Sweetheart tree

Rich, ruby red 'Mercedes' roses and the natural shades of white sea lavender (*Limonium*, also known as statice) create this luxurious and romantic tree.

The trunk is made up of three branches encrusted with lichen. Around it I have wound a writhing length of thorny vine to create interest and movement.

All topiary trees such as this are made in the same way. You will need a container, some plaster of Paris, newspaper, and a plastic bag to begin. Your trunk can be found on any woodland walk or from the prunings of your own yard. However, trunks are deceptively long, so measure yours out against the container first.

Line the container with a little crumpled newspaper, then open out the plastic bag to accommodate the plaster. Mix the plaster of Paris according to the instructions on the pack and half-fill the plastic bag. Take your premeasured trunk and plunge it into the plaster, spooning the remaining mixture around the trunk base. Leave it to dry, checking it periodically, so that the trunk does not lean over too much.

My plaster took only ten minutes to become firm, but I then left it overnight to dry out completely.

Some plaster expands on drying, so the crumpled newspaper will accommodate this.

For the next step, you will need a large sphere of florist foam and a glue gun. Push the foam down hard onto the trunk, gouging out some of the foam to make a hollow for the trunk. When you are happy with the positioning, glue the foam onto the trunk, pushing it down firmly until the arrangement feels secure, as the foam will be taking the weight of the display.

Taking your roses and sea lavender, begin by measuring the height of the first stem at the top of the sphere. All the other pieces will need to be planted to this height to give the tree a round appearance. So, with a pair of sharp scissors, begin trimming and planting a section at a time. Push the stems straight into the foam to prevent them from crossing.

Occasionally, step back to assess your progress. If you notice an empty space, gently ease a flower in the gap to fill it.

Once the head is complete, finish the base by packing a cushion of moss around the trunk.

*This topiary tree uses an abundant ingredient: sea lavender. Readily available and inexpensive, the sea lavender creates a lacy, white background for the glorious rich, red roses. Make the trunk of the tree more interesting by twisting a vine around it before setting it into the base.*

*Line the container with crumpled paper and a plastic bag. Half-fill the bag with plaster of Paris and insert the trunk. Top up the plaster and leave it to dry.*

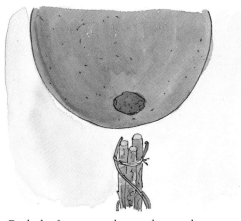

*Push the foam onto the trunk to make an impression. Gouge out a little of the foam to make a hole. Glue the trunk in the hole, pushing the two firmly together.*

# Pastel tree

Warm peach and pastel greens combine beautifully in the head of this tree. To achieve the best balance, use more of one ingredient than the other, even if the ratio is small. Here, there are slightly more poppy heads than roses. For an extra feature which gives additional interest, create a small frill of another ingredient at the bottom of the head. I have tucked in sea lavender.

Choose pretty pastel shades of peach and the palest green or similar colors to complement your decor. I made this arrangement for a dinner party and placed paper-wrapped macaroons around the trunk for delicious after-dinner nibbling.

This tree is made in the same way as the Sweetheart Tree, but as the head is busier, it has a short, simple trunk.

The head is made from 'Gerdo' roses and poppy (*Papaver*) seedheads and, like the previous tree, built up in sections. Do not strip off all the foliage from the roses as it helps to fill in any gaps.

Finish the Pastel tree with the smallest amount of peachy sea lavender (*Limonium*) inserted underneath the tree to form a frilly little "petticoat."

# Egg tree

Eggs really interest me. Their fascinating ovoid shape and differing hues of pale pinkish yellows, warm beiges, and bronzed skin tones offer unusual potential.

I made the base and trunk as for the Sweetheart Tree, but here I used a larger foam sphere.

There are 92 hens' eggs in this arrangement and, as each one has to be blown, my daughters soon tired of omelettes and soufflés.

I discovered the most convenient way to make any arrangement involving large numbers of eggs was to build them up gradually. Blowing one or two eggs is one thing; blowing 92 is quite another!

Striking, fascinating, and sensual, this extraordinary topiary tree is made from ordinary brown eggs. Each egg must be blown and wired, with the addition of a pretty glass bead, before it can be set into the tree head. Violet and peach colors work well with the natural colors of eggs; I have used violet reindeer moss in the base and pale peach as a background color for the foam.

The easiest way to blow an egg is to take a large needle or hat pin and push it through the length of the egg. Gently ease away a little eggshell from the pin prick at the blunt end of the egg and blow from the pointed end.

After a few attempts, you will soon become as practiced as me.

Once you have assembled your eggs and basic tree, you will need to gather together some beige or pale peach latex paint, medium-gauge stub wire, pretty glass beads, reindeer moss, and an Easter chick or two.

As gaps on this arrangement will be unavoidable, paint the foam sphere in a pale flesh color. Once it is dry, you can begin.

Take an 8-inch length of stub wire and thread the first 1¼-inches through your bead. Double the wire back on itself and twist the two ends together right up to the bead.

Now thread the beaded wire from the pointed end of the egg through to the blunt end. You will be left with a wire "tail." Bend this "tail" back on itself to double it, so that when you push the wired egg into the foam sphere, the wire will not buckle.

Using the wired eggs, start at the top of the tree, as usual, and progress down the sides, nestling one egg up against another.

For the base of the tree, I disguised the plaster with light violet-colored reindeer moss and added two chicks and a few painted eggs.

I adore this little folly, but even if you are not enamored of it, it does demonstrate the interesting use of eggs in floral arrangements.

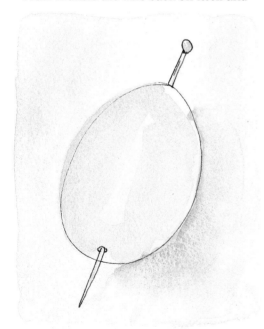

*Push a hat pin or large needle through the length of the egg. Then gently ease away a little shell from the blunt end by wiggling the pin. Blow from the pointed end, and the contents will empty out of the larger hole at the blunt end.*

*Thread 1¼ inches of an 8-inch-long stub wire through a bead. Bring the wire back on itself and twist the two ends together right up to the bead. Now thread the beaded wire through the pointed end of the egg down to the blunt end.*

# Teasel tree

This little tree is made with the fruits of a blustery seashore walk with my young daughters. Had we not been gathering, we would not have walked so long or so far.

The basic tree is made just like the others, using just one rather short, thick trunk and a large cone of florist foam. It is planted in an ordinary weathered flowerpot.

To decorate the basic tree, you will need to gather teasels (*Dipsacus sylvestris*) of differing sizes.

They are mixed with soft rush (*Juncus effusus*) which grows in wet and marshy ground. Despite its name, soft rush has a hard, dark dried seedpod with a vicious spike and spears of leaves which look very attractive darting out from the outline of this display.

Nodding thistles (*Carduus nutans*) and a natural jute ribbon complete this arrangement.

Sort the teasels into large and small sizes. You will need the smaller ones for the top and the largest ones for the base of the tree to give it visual weight.

Begin at the top of the tree, inserting a teasel, then progress down the cone, planting the teasels alternated with rush to fill in the gaps.

Underneath the cone, plant a soft rush petticoat.

Fill in the base of the pot with nodding thistles, or you could use husks of beech nuts (*Fagus grandifolia*) or even crumbled bark.

Finally, take the soft rush leaves and place them strategically throughout the display. Tie a jute ribbon around the base as a soft contrast.

*This natural-style Teasel tree – with its dusty browns and rich earthy colors – is a complete contrast to the other topiary trees.*

# WREATHS & GARLANDS

*The traditional woven wreath is centuries old. Representing the perpetual renewing of the seasons, the wreath is used for tribute, memorial, and celebration, and it is another means of displaying nature's fruits within the home. The selection of wreaths in this chapter offer some ideas with which you can experiment. Create your own Celebration garland, using summer flowers, grasses, pine cones, or different media such as feathers or shells.*

*Two basic methods are used to create these wreaths: the Celebration, Summer, and Herb wreaths are constructed using a florist foam circle. The Autumn wreath is very easily achieved by twisting natural materials together.*

# Summer splendor garland

Combine bright, vibrant purples and pinks to make a summer's garland.

This design is worked on a florist foam circle, in the same way as the Celebration Garland and Herb Wreath, but the choice of materials gives an entirely different effect to hang on your wall or door.

The success of this garland depends on grouping the elements together so that they retain their individual characters. Try to avoid "scattering" ingredients, as the end result will be a rather messy blur.

The principal flowers are roses, hydrangea, and deep-lilac statice (*Limonium sinuatum*). To these rather rounded forms, I added bunches of barley (*Hordeum*) and fluffy hare's tail grass (*Lagurus ovatus*) to give length and movement. For contrasting texture I selected two slightly exotic ingredients: rattan palm (*Calamus*) and white-tipped cones. For depth and infill, I used spiral eucalyptus leaves (*Eucalyptus pulverulenta*) and scraps of rose foliage.

A large paper bow was the only other element.

Paper ribbon is a wonderful complement to dried flowers, reflecting their more subtle tones and hues. It can be bought from stationers or florists in tightly coiled lengths. Simply rub the coil between your thumbs and fingers to unravel it to its full width, then treat it the way you would fabric ribbon.

The other advantage of paper ribbon is that it holds its shape well when tied into a bow.

It is with the ribbon that I began my garland. As the bow is so full, I tied it around the foam circle first.

I then began folding my barley in half to give me both ears and stalks together and secured two hearty clusters with florist tape. I pushed one cluster into the foam beneath the bow.

Many people associate wreaths and garlands with winter decorations. This display is a tribute to summer with its pretty pinks and purples and the rich clusters of roses. The wonderful blue-green bow is made from paper ribbon; it is the perfect complement to the eucalyptus, hydrangea, and rose leaves. Clusters of wheat and fluffy hare's tail grass give movement to an otherwise static arrangement.

*Vibrant purple statice sits next to cerise pink roses. This garland works well because each ingredient is set into the circle in groups. For ease, gather each cluster and bind it with tape before inserting it into the foam. This gives a much better effect than if you try to insert the ingredients individually.*

*Fold three or four stems of barley or wheat in half to give you both stalks and ears together. Bind the fold with tape before pushing it into the foam.*

Underneath the barley, I inserted one hydrangea head. Take care with hydrangeas as the tiny florets break off easily. If you buy hydrangea heads, they are usually wired with stub wire. This makes them stronger and easier to insert into the foam. However, if you take care, you can push them in by their own stems.

Behind this, at the edge of the garland, push in a few sprays of rose leaves.

Continue working around the garland in a clockwise direction. Tuck a little statice next to the hydrangea, then insert three or four deep crimson roses.

Push in a large cluster of rattan palm just above and beyond the roses. The cones sit below this, and these will need wiring before inserting them into the foam. (Full instructions for wiring cones appear on page 115.)

Continue around with a clump of hare's

tail grass; bunch this together and bind it with tape before inserting it in to the foam. Next, tuck in more statice and another cluster of barley. In among them, gently push in three bright red roses.

As you work, continue to assess your progress for weight, density, color, and texture combinations.

Where there are gaps, tuck in small sprays of rose leaves. These are excellent for filling in, adding a contrast of texture and color.

Make two more bunches of fluffy hare's tail grass and insert them close to each other at the next section. In among this nestle a pink rose.

Come up the side of the garland with a profusion of eucalyptus and rose leaves. Among this mass of blue-greens, nestle three more pink roses and, toward the top, a large cluster of statice.

Finally, work the remaining section of the garland with eight or nine smaller pink roses, inserting them so that they sweep up from the bow.

At the top, tucked in behind the bow, push another cluster of hare's tail grass and a little sprig of hydrangea.

*It is often effective to add a little touch of the unusual to your displays. Here, a complete contrast of tone and texture is supplied by the bobbly rattan palm and white tipped, furry cones.*

# Herb wreath

If you are a lover of cooking or gardening, this herb wreath is a delight for the kitchen. Although the atmosphere in most kitchens is too moist for floral displays, this wreath – as a practical kitchen aid – can last quite well, providing you use the herbs fairly quickly, as they tend to lose their flavor.

Gather your herbs from the garden or buy them from a good supplier. I was fortunate to pick my herbs from the rocky hills of Provence in the May sunshine.

The main herbs I have used are thyme, rosemary in flower (although flowering herbs are usually past their best, rosemary flowers look so attractive) and tarragon, with garlic and cinnamon to decorate. They are inserted into a florist foam circle. Stub wire and a little natural raffia are the only other requirements.

As herbs shed their delicate leaves easily, I cropped mine to the length I needed – about 4 inches – before drying them. This I did by hanging them and leaving them overnight. Try to avoid unnecessary movement of the herbs once they are dry because they do become more brittle.

Cut the rosemary flower heads down to 2 inches and put to one side. Then take the rosemary leaves on their robust wooden stems and sink each one into the outer edge of the foam at a 45° angle, working around the circle clockwise.

Now insert rosemary into the inside of the circle, once again working clockwise.

Build up the wreath by inserting the light feathery tarragon over the foam to fill in between the rosemary. I left two cresent areas free to insert the rosemary flower heads and the delicate thyme.

When the whole of the foam circle is completely covered, you are ready to add the garlic and cinnamon.

Cut the cinnamon to 2 inches – you will need six lengths. I then took three sticks and bent a long piece of wire around them, twisting it together to secure the cinnamon tightly.

To disguise the wire and add interest, cover it with a little raffia secured with a knot.

Take one wired cinnamon bunch and plunge the wire through the herbs and the foam, splaying the wires out on the back of the foam ring for additional security.

Slightly overlap the second cinnamon bunch over the first to add depth and interest to the arrangement.

The garlic bulbs will also need wiring before adding them to the wreath. Push the wire straight through the bulb and twist both ends of the wire to secure it.

Attach the heavier garlic to the base of the wreath. Pick out two or three cloves on the second bulb before wiring it into the wreath. Once again, this adds interest to the finished display.

These herbs and spices can then be plucked for cooking and replaced when convenient.

*Never underestimate the value of herbs and spices for your floral displays. Here, a complete wreath has been constructed from culinary herbs and ingredients. The advantage of this display is that it has a practical function, too. If you do intend to use the wreath for culinary purposes, you will need to replenish it frequently, as herbs lose their aroma quickly in the moist atmosphere of a kitchen.*

*Once you have cut the cinnamon sticks to the desired length, bunch three or four together and wind a piece of wire around them. Cover the wire with raffia.*

# Celebration garland

This fabulous tribute to winter is an interesting variation on more traditional wreaths. It needs quite a lot of preparation, but the finished result renders this more than worthwhile.

The wreath is formed on a foam circle. Other items you must gather together include boughs of spruce (*Picea*) – the type of Christmas tree which does not shed its needles so quickly – a good selection of mixed nuts, cardamom, cloves, small and large pine cones, a variety of ribbon, a dozen quails' eggs, and three or four miniature baskets. To secure everything, you will also require plenty of stub wire and a glue gun.

Begin by preparing the tiny baskets. I got the really miniature baskets from a doll supply outlet; many good toy stores sell them or try a quality florist shop.

The slightly larger baskets are certainly available from florists or department stores.

Take the tiniest basket first and wire it through the base as shown. Wire the other basket through its side. This will give it an interesting tilt when wired to the foam circle.

Fill one basket with cardamon and the other with cloves, securing the spices with the aid of a glue gun.

Now take the other little baskets and wire them in the same way. Fill one with hazelnuts and the other with small almonds, again using your glue gun.

Put the baskets on one side.

Although something of a luxury, the speckled shells of quails' eggs really adds to the splendor of this wreath. As each egg needs blowing and wiring (instructions appear on page 114), save the contents for an haute cuisine omelette!

Once you have blown and wired the eggs, put them too, on one side.

Now work on the individual bunches of

This Celebration garland is a lovely variation on the more traditional Christmas wreath. Cones, gold-trimmed scarlet ribbon, and Christmas tree boughs are all here, but the unusual addition of quails' eggs, cinnamon sticks, and nut clusters give this garland a more stylish note.

nuts and spices. Wire together cinnamon sticks; I made three bunches altogether.

For the groups of nuts, I used chestnuts, walnuts, and brazil nuts. Rather than drill holes in the nuts to wire them to the wreath, glue several nuts together with the glue gun and slip the wire easily through the complete group. Perhaps this is cheating a little, but drilling holes without specialized tools is a tricky business.

Use this tip to assemble and wire the small pine cones. The larger cones can be wired individually, as shown.

Finally, tie some bows using ribbons of different colors and textures: I have used reds, greens, and gold.

You are now ready to begin constructing the wreath.

Take the foam circle and sink into it 2-inch pieces of spruce. Do this in a random way to create a sense of movement.

Experiment with the position of the materials first before you wire them into the circle. Start with the baskets; keep the heavier ones near the base and tuck in

other things to see how the different elements work together. Place some of the ribbons at the edges of the wreath as this looks most effective.

Occasionally, stand back from the wreath to assess your progress. Sometimes I find I become too engrossed with my work, which takes on a very different appearance when viewed from a distance.

When you are confident with the positioning of all the ingredients, wire all the items through the foam, splaying the wire out at the back of the wreath for added security.

As a final element, you can add sprigs of catkins around the perimeter of the wreath for a little additional movement. Fine, feathery twigs work as well if you are unable to find any catkins.

Before you hang your wreath, make sure everything is wired on tightly; you do not want bits falling off every time you bang the door!

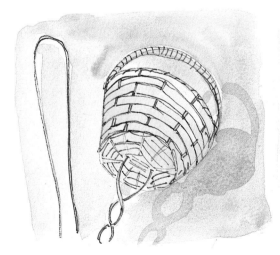

*I tend to use medium gauge stub wire for everything except really heavy items. Bend the wire into a hairpin shape and push it down through the basket leaving long enough tails to go through the foam circle and out the back.*

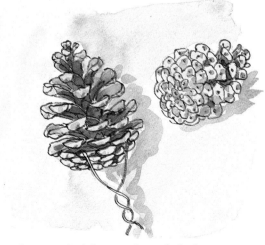

*Push one end of the wire through the lowest band of scales and out the other side, leaving a little wire protruding. Push this wire back around the cone and twist the two tails of wire together, bringing them under the cone to form a stem.*

The success of this garland relies on the contrasting textures and complementary tones all held together by the scarlet bows. Shiny nuts are echoed by the glitzy ribbon; the rough and rugged texture of the brazil nuts, cinnamon, and fir cones balance well against them, while the pale, speckled eggs lighten the display.

Cut the spruce into small 2-inch pieces and strip the ends of their needles to give you a stem on each piece. Push the spruce into the foam circle randomly to give the garland a feeling of movement.

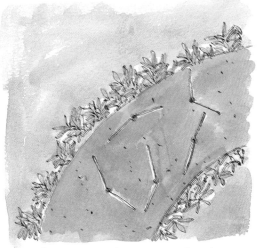

Do make sure everything is secured to the foam circle. It is best to wire every item with long enough "tails" which can be pushed through the foam and out the back. The tails can then be splayed out for extra security.

# Kiss of autumn wreath

A walk on a crisp fall day inspired this charming, medieval-style wreath.

Seeing overgrown blackberry vines, ferns, and copper leaves in the hedge, I plucked a few, adding some shining rose hips later on. As I walked, I twisted the vine – complete with its leaves – into a hoop as it was much easier to carry that way; and so this autumn wreath took shape.

At home, I stood all the leaves and ferns in a glycerin solution (40% glycerin to 60% very hot water) and left them overnight. Although it changes the color of the leaves, it does mean you can use them as you would any dried ingredient: they will no longer crack.

The next day, I was ready to begin. I laid the vine hoop on a flat surface and examined the ingredients I had gathered: English oak leaves (*Quercus robur*), copper beech (*Fagus sylvatica*), Guelder rose leaves (*Viburnum opulus*), spikemoss (*Selaginella*), fern, and rose hips. To this, I added *Leucodendron plumosum*, reindeer moss, and dyed broom bloom or nipplewort (*Laspana communis*).

The oak leaves form natural clusters on their twigs, so these I simply inserted into the base of the hoop.

Next, I gathered the rose hips into three separate bunches, bound their stems with tape, and then inserted my wire. These I pushed into the wreath in the center of the oak.

The larger leaves, the Guelder rose, also needed to be taped into a cluster, then wired. These I added to the upper left-hand side of the hoop.

Beneath the Guelder rose, I nestled two *Leucodendron plumosum*, wiring them as I would a pine cone. They add a delightful contrast in texture.

Copper beech leaves in small clusters came next and I covered the base of the stems with some natural reindeer moss.

I now completed this side of the circle using a fat bunch of clubmoss. (This I picked from the base of a tree, you can use any small, soft fern-like foliage though).

To finish the wreath, come up the right hand side with some red and green dyed broom bloom and a few fern leaves.

Fill in any naked parts with small fern leaves, always echoing the flowing movement of the wreath.

*A triumph of texture and rich colors, this simple wreath is easily made by twisting the vine into a hoop and slipping in other ingredients. The oak and Guelder rose leaves need to be preserved in glycerin first to retain their suppleness. The luster that these leaves develop is a lovely contrast to the dull green of the blackberry leaves. Shiny rose hips add weight and color at the bottom of the hoop.*

*Gather rose hips into three separate clusters, bind them with tape, and push them into the twisted hoop of blackberry vine and oak leaves.*

# SWAGS & PENDANTS

*Probably the most elaborate and
ornate of floral displays, swags and
pendants are glorious tributes to
most grand occasions.*

*In this chapter I have given
instructions for three quite different
creations. The magnificent Festive
Table Swag boasts a richness and
splendor reminiscent of a huge
Renaissance feast day. The softer
pastels of the Glorious Summer
Pendant and Swag would delight
any bridal couple and their guests at
the reception. Finally, the
Thanksgiving Drop, is an exciting
and slightly unusual wall hanging
for the fall.*

*Although these projects can appear
daunting to tackle, their chief
requirements – once you have
assembled enough materials – are
nimble fingers and patience.*

# Festive table swag

Laden with summer's late glories and the heady fruits of dappled autumn days, this sumptuous floral swag boasts an abundance of nature's riches.

To create a feeling of movement, vitality and surprise, the choice of fruits and flowers – and their juxtaposition to one another – is extremely important.

Here, I have decorated a small table with a swag of materials of varying tones and textures. I have used some fairly exotic varieties, but felt that the design and occasion warranted something a little special. Good dried-flower suppliers should be able to obtain the more unusual items, but this is a good example where you can experiment with other materials of your choice.

Gourds and carline thistles (*Carlina acaulis*) form the focal points of the swag; quails' eggs, baby corn or maize (*Zea mays*), cocoa pods, and Badam (an interesting Indian seedpod) add contrasting texture, while Chinese lanterns (*Physalis alkekengi*) and *Protea compacta* fill in the outline. Superb heavy ribbon and gigantic tassels complete the display.

The mechanics the swag are based on include florist foam, string, chicken wire, stub wire, a glue gun, and felt. Nails and a hammer will be necessary to secure the swag to the underside of the table if the one you are decorating is large and makeshift. However, if you are using a good piece of furniture, it is best to lash it tightly to the table leg with string and sew the swag through the cloth with strong thread. Do not, however, secure a heavy swag using this method.

*Create this sumptuous swag for a special banquet or party. The swollen gourds, bursting corn, and fiery Chinese lanterns create a look of abundance and opulence.*

*Rich colors and exotic contours are the key to this swag's success. Corn and cocoa provide length and movement, while gourds and Chinese lanterns give substance and warm hues. The quails' eggs offset all the other ingredients with their wonderful speckled shells.*

To judge the length and depth of the swag, I draped a piece of string along the table and cut it when I was satisfied with the effect.

When you have established the size of your swag, lay the string on a flat work surface and take two bricks of foam. Place one brick in the center of the string and cut the other in two, placing a piece on each side.

Now take a piece of each wire and mold it around the foam to form a swag. I tested mine against the table, remembering that the finished swag would be laden with materials.

Firmly secure the wire edges by intertwining them together and twisting them back into the foam.

Cut a piece of felt the size and shape of the swag and glue it to the back of the wire. This will help prevent damage to your furniture.

Now the fun begins. Before you insert anything into the swag, you must gather all your ingredients together.

First, wire the heavy items such as the corn (maize) and gourds.

The quails' eggs will need to be blown and wired with a glass bead. Instructions to do this are given on page 114.

Once you have assembled several clusters of eggs, put them to one side. I used three dozen, nearly 40 eggs! However, they do make the most heavenly omelette.

Wire the baby maize and double-wire the heaviest gourds. This will give the gourds additional security and prevent them from slipping in the wrong direction.

The best way to wire these weighty fruits is to bore a hole through them and out the other side with a skewer. Push two pieces of stub wire through the holes and twist the ends together.

If the gourds are very heavy, it is best to wire them in two places. Simply bore another hole a little higher up the side of the fruit and insert more wire.

From the ribbon, form a rosette. This is easily done by pleating the ribbon folds one against the other. Push a wire through the folds to secure them; by twisting the ribbon slightly, the folds fall open into a rosette.

Attach the rosette to the beginning of the wire frame and wrap the ribbon round and round the swag, finishing at the other end with another rosette.

Take six giant tassels and drape three from each rosette, securing them from behind with wire pushed into the mesh frame. Pleat parts of the cord holding the tassel to give additional movement within the rosette, and trail some cord over the ribbon to enhance the interesting texture.

Having wrapped the wire frame with ribbon and cord, I then attached it to a wall to work.

Begin centrally with the gourds, tilting them against one another and tucking the open baby maize in behind them to complete a focal triangle.

Wedge an intriguing badam seedpod beneath the central point, pushing in more wired baby maize behind to serve as a background.

Work from the center out, placing clusters of quails' eggs, another badam, and trails of cocoa pods flowing toward the outer edges.

In against the egg clusters tuck groups of Chinese lanterns with their brilliant orange hues and contrast the texture with straw-like carline thistles. (Be wary of exactly where you place them, as extracting them can be painful!)

On the left-hand side, I have added a group of smaller gourds to balance the display, and tucked in *Protea compacta* to help strengthen the outline.

Last, I wired trailing cocoa pods and added them in among the tassels.

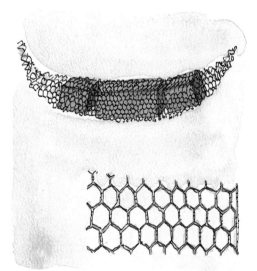

*Place one brick of foam in the center of the chicken wire. Cut another brick in half and place one on each side of the first brick. Now wrap the wire up around the foam and mold it into a swag shape.*

*Use a skewer to bore a hole through the gourd in two places. Push heavy-duty stub wire through the holes and twist the ends together. If the fruit is very heavy, bore another hole and wire it twice.*

# Summer swag & pendant

Perfect for a wedding, christening, or mid-summer's party, this splendid, colorful display evokes the summer's sun and warm, balmy days.

Any swag can be adapted, as here, to create an additional pendant. Although time-consuming, the overall effect is magnificent.

Begin by gathering together string, blocks and scraps of florist foam, chicken wire, and wire cutters.

Using a length of string, measure against your table or wall the length and depth of the swag and adjoining pendant.

Using the string as a guide, cut out two pieces of chicken wire, one for the swag and one for the pendant.

I spread the chicken wire out on a work surface and filled it with cut bricks of foam. I then wrapped the wire around the foam and wrestled with it, molding it into the shapes required.

Do turn all the chicken wire ends into the foam, as they can snag your hand badly when you are arranging.

For this project, I hung the wire forms from a window ledge to give me a better idea of the finished product. However, you can, of course, lay the wire forms on a flat work surface if you prefer.

Begin with the pendant.

For this I used globe artichokes (*Cynara scolymus*), various *Nigella*, hydrangea, strawflowers (*Helichrysum bracteatum*), poppy heads (*Papaver*), roses, peonies (*Paeonia lactiflora*), delphinium, *Protea compacta* buds, and lavender. Some of these need to be taped and wired before inserting them into the form.

I adored the fluffy pompons, or "chokes" from the artichoke, and decided to position them prominently as one of the focal points of the display.

Beneath them I wired artichokes in their more familiar form, and then I

This magnificent swag and pendant of beautiful summer pastels uses a fabulous combination of old-fashioned country flowers and two rather exotic varieties: the globe artichoke and Protea buds. You do not need to use exactly the same flowers in both pendant and swag, but you should stick to the main forms, colors, and textures. For example, the "chokes" are used only in the pendant, but their creamy color is echoed in the swag.

worked down the pendant with the pink *Protea compacta* buds.

For additional depth and substance, I squeezed pale pink peony flowers in on each side of the "chokes," positioning one slightly below the pompons.

Unlike a traditional flower arrangement where it is more customary to form the outline first and then work on the focal points, these wired forms have their outline already established, so you can happily play around with the larger pieces before working on the other elements and filling in.

I next built up the background using different textures. Clusters of small red roses I bound with tape and pushed them directly into the foam strategically throughout the pendant. They give a slightly mottled appearance when set in against the other materials.

Poppy heads give another texture and hue to the pendant, and these I also taped into a cluster before inserting them into the foam.

Make the most of the pink dephiniums. I cut them down and used the dominant flowerheads in the foreground, and filled in behind with the smaller flowers from the lower part of the stem. They are an important, although not prevailing, part of the display, interspersed in clumps throughout the pendant. Cluster some delphiniums with a little lavender; the colors are a perfect complement to each other.

I then worked down the side with clumps of *Nigella orientalis* and filled in the background with love-in-a-mist and hydrangea heads. The hydrangea in particular provides good cover for the foam base.

Toward the top of the display, I dotted in some pretty pink-tipped *Helichrysum* or strawflowers, keeping to one side of the pendant.

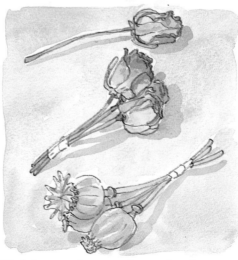

Bind clusters of roses and poppy heads together at the base of the stems with tape. This makes it much easier to push them into the foam.

*The delightful fluffy "chokes" (**above**) – of the globe artichoke – immediately catch the eye. **Right**: The pendant is given length and movement with the clever positioning of artichokes and Protea buds, which sweep down from the center. These spiky shapes are echoed on the other side of the pendant by the star-shaped Nigella orientalis. Softening these angular shapes are the soft forms of red roses nestling amid lavender topped with clusters of delphinium.*

Finally, I worked the upper and lower edges with stems of lavender. (I sprayed them first with some firm-hold hairspray, as in this position they so easily shed their flowers.)

With the pendant complete, you can turn your attentions to the swag.

Continue the theme of the pendant, using the same basic materials. Once again, I used artichokes as my focal point; here, using three large heads, one in deep purple flower. They must be wired twice through the base before inserting them into the chicken wire. For added strength, twist the stub wire through the chicken wire and not just into the foam. This is advisable for all heavy or unstable items.

I then tucked one deep pink peony in among the artichokes, placing others around the perimeter of this central group.

Extend outward with the long forms of the *Protea compacta* buds, keeping them close to the center of the swag. I reserved six buds, however, placing three at each end of the display.

Once these dominant features are in place, filling in is easy and fun.

I wired together separate clusters of lavender, poppy heads, cream and pink roses, and love-in-a-mist. Make some clusters really substantial to give the swag fullness and rich opulence.

I used the hydrangea heads to tuck in around the edges and cover the floral foam.

Strawflowers in varying shades of pink were dotted strategically throughout the display. Among the lavender, or between the artichokes, these merry little flower heads give importance and contrast to the other elements.

Stand back from the display to see if anything needs adjusting. Remember, nothing here is irreversible; you can always pop things in, then take them out if you do not like the effect.

# Thanksgiving drop

Gathering the maturing fruits of summer into this ripe decoration create a rustic, yet slightly wild, arrangement.

The wire structure is made from floral foam, bound with chicken wire in the same way as the Summer Pendant.

I worked this pendant in situ, as the colors and texture of the brick wall on which the pendant was to hang directly influenced my choice of materials.

The main elements of the pendant are gourds. These are available from most dried-flower suppliers in various sizes, colors, and forms. Wheat (*Triticum aestivum*), corn, or maize (*Zea mays*), chili peppers, bell reed, and spiral cane cones constitute the other materials.

The heavier gourds will need substantial wiring before they can be used. Bore two holes through them, as explained on page 115, first.

The larger corn or maize will need heavy-gauge wire inserted through it twice before you can use it. For the smaller corn, you need only wire once through the base. Peel back the outer leaves of the corn to reveal the cob beneath.

To begin, place the largest gourds into good focal positions. I chose to make two groups of gourds. As they are so heavy, it is best to wrap the stub wire through and around the chicken wire, rather than just inserting it into the floral foam.

Then position the corn against the gourds, working with the largest ones first, angling them out into slender fan shapes. Insert the smaller corn beneath their larger counterparts, following the lines of the bigger pieces.

Now take the wheat and gently bend each piece in two, taking care as the stems can easily snap. Lay a piece of wire in the fold of the wheat, pull the wire together and twist the ends securely.

Insert the wheat, encouraging it to flow

downward and outward from the corn and gourds, until you reach the base of the arrangement.

For the upper part of the display, cut shorter lengths of wheat.

Use up any broken stems by inserting them roguishly throughout the display. These give the pendant a rather alarming appearance and are in stark contrast to the wheat ears which soften the outline. The overall impression is therefore one of slight abandon.

At this point, step back from the display to assess your progress and evaluate which parts now need work.

Fill in some gaps with clusters of spiky red chili peppers. They create a pleasing contrast of color between the areas of gourds.

Spiraling cane cones throughout the form, add to the slight wildness of the piece.

Finally, give the arrangement depth by filling in with bell reed.

Bold and striking, this harvest pendant is filled with traditional fall produce arranged in a contemporary style. Wheat and barley stalks are made as much use of as the ears themselves. The spiky stalks give the pendant a slightly abandoned appearance. **Far left**: clusters of bright red chili peppers provide an unusual infill, but their devil-red colors and wonderful long, twisted bodies add a fascinating element and complement so well the curly spirals of the canes.

# FREE
# FORMS

*The surprise element has become
increasingly fashionable in floral
displays, so be willing to
experiment.*

*Dried flowers, with their
contrasting tonal qualities and
inspirational textures, provide an
ideal medium in which to exercise
free expression. However, most free
forms are created with careful
planning and an eye to proportion
and color, so do not think free form
means random disorder!*

*In this chapter, I have allowed
flowers to meander across a basket
and a candle sconce; I have
experimented with unusual
containers such as a large verdigris
platter; I have also let the subject or
setting play a key role in the
display. With free forms, empty
space can be as much a part of the
design as the object it surrounds.*

*Flowers lend themselves to
discovery, so let your imagination
flow. Use these ideas to inspire you
to try others.*

# Lavender urn

Strength and substance are not qualities you would expect from fragile, gentle lavender. Yet in this striking display, the shape and quantity of lavender create a dense purple-gray bush. It is beautiful in summer for the hearth, or nearby in the winter, when the warmth from the fire will release the essential oils and fill the room with perfume.

This design can be adapted or translated using another long-stemmed flower or grass, but if you wish to retain this shape and status, it is important to maintain the proportions: one-third container to two-thirds floral material.

Place a brick of florist foam upright in your container and wedge more pieces down the sides so that there is no possibility of movement. A tall display such as this can become rather unwieldy, especially if you have to move it.

Now glue another brick of foam on top of the first one. You will need to make this arrangement extra secure by plunging a bamboo stick or garden cane through both bricks, as glue is not enough to keep them in place.

Now slowly but surely, and very patiently, stick each piece of lavender into the foam, judging the length of each one before you insert it, keeping the overall shape in mind as you work. It is not advisable to bunch the stems together before inserting them, as this does not achieve the same effect.

I put my container on a revolving cake plate as this helped in the construction.

Imagine the finished shape to be like an ovoid sphere, and work one segment at a time from top to bottom.

To avoid damaging the lavender on the last segment, gently push back the surrounding stems with one hand and hold them until you have inserted the new pieces.

Once you have finished, trim any disobedient pieces with sharp scissors to make sure you maintain your outline.

*The classic lines of this Lavender urn make a most charming and elegant showpiece for your home. Despite its simple form, it is quite painstaking to construct, as each stem must be placed individually. However, the finished result renders the effort worthwhile.*

*Wedge a brick of foam into your container by squeezing smaller pieces of foam down the sides. Now glue another brick of foam on top of the first and secure with a stick.*

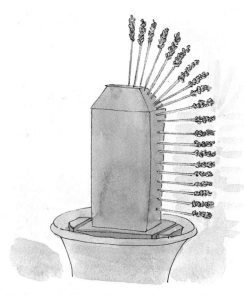

*Each piece of lavender must be inserted individually. Work one section at a time, from top to bottom, keeping the overall shape in mind.*

# Summer flower basket

A very traditional design, this beautiful basket is bursting with all the delicate hues of summer.

It is the color scheme that is the secret to this basket's success. Warm pink and apricot, pale peach and cream, alongside rich, old golds; all nestle together in complete harmony.

Any flowers which complement each other in this way will work well. However, as a guide, I have used delphinium in ice-cream pink, cream and peach-toned strawflowers (*Helichrysum bracteatum*), love-in-a-mist (*Nigella damascena*), sneezewort or pearly achillea (*Achillea ptarmica*), and a little foliage. Floral foam is the only other requirement.

Secure the foam inside the base of the basket and organize your ingredients according to length and movement. I made a pile of curved stems, whatever the flower, saving the straight stems to stand upright next to the handle.

In order to achieve the rounded curve which echoes the basket's natural shape, I planted a "parting of flowers" along the center, from the rim to the handle and down the other side. This gave me the outline of the curve.

Remember that the pretty pearl achillea are quite delicate, so try to insert these first in each section, as their stems break very easily.

Beginning at the handle, I worked on one area at a time, gradually spreading down one side of the basket, avoiding poking flowers in among a cluster, for fear of breaking the ones already standing.

Do allow just enough room around the handle to pick the basket up.

Work the straight stems first, pushing them into the foam a section at a time. Use the curved stems to curve gently over the basket rim and add a little fern or foliage here to soften the outline.

Work the other side of the basket, repeating the same pattern.

A most traditional basket, this summer flower display can use any number of pastel colors to achieve this effect. Although the design appears to meander, it is carefully constructed, with straight-stemmed flowers forming a "center part" around the handle and curved stems fanning down to the basket's rim. One side is worked first, then the other follows the same pattern. **Far left**: allow the flowers to overlap the handle, but allow enough room to hold the basket.

# Kitchen basket with bread

This delightful kitchen folly is fun and entertaining and a perfect distraction if you are pursued into the kitchen!

The wheat ears soften the outline and are a perfect contrast to the heavier breads, while the long stalks are echoed in the lengthy forms of the French loaf and breadsticks.

Gather together your materials: a variety of bread, buns, breadsticks, and rolls. You will also need common wheat (*Triticum aestivum*), black-eared barley (*Hordeum*), and a large basket. Clear varnish is necessary to preserve the bread and give the display a glossy sheen. You will also need your ever-useful glue gun and a large paper bow to trim the complete arrangement.

Take a selection of breads and hollow them out by making a small hole in the base of each one and easing the contents out. My daughters helped with their small fingers.

Place the larger loaves in the base of the basket, tilting them at angles until you are happy with the result. Then pile the lighter buns and plaited rolls or bagels on top. Try to keep the items at varying angles to add interest, but do not feel everything has to interlink; sometimes empty spaces are also interesting.

For height, use the French loaf and breadsticks.

Look at the display from several vantage points, and also in situ if you are placing it on a shelf or countertop.

*Bread displays have become increasingly fashionable, but you do not have to buy special loaves and buns. All the items in this lovely kitchen basket I preserved myself. Use as wide a variety of breads as possible: breadsticks, buns, rolls, and various loaves look wonderful when varnished and set into a basket of wheat.*

When you are satisfied with the effect of the display, begin to glue the hollowed-out bread into position. Now leave the bread for two or three days to become stale. Coat all the bread surfaces with varnish, adding a sprinkle of poppy seeds to some items if you wish; they easily stick to the wet varnish. Leave the complete display to dry overnight.

To complete the arrangement, gently bend stems of wheat and barley in the center so they form a tight V shape. This way you have both stalk and ear for use; they give height and movement to an otherwise squat arrangement.

Now glue clumps of barley and wheat into the display. You can bind them into clusters first with a little natural raffia or tape.

Add a ravishing bow of paper ribbon, and your kitchen folly is complete.

*Scoop out as much bread as possible through a hole in the base. This will prevent it from becoming moldy.*

# Roses cast in bronze

The simplicity of this mound of roses set against the turquoise-green of the dish is extraordinary. The bowl itself is quite a feature, but the roses enhance its beauty.

A round piece of florist foam, a large stone, and deep red roses are all that are required for this design.

Embed a stone in the foam to prevent the rose mound from slipping around.

Now simply insert the roses, cutting their stems short, to create a little mound or hillock in the center of the bowl.

One of the simplest, yet most effective, displays in the book, the design does require a quantity of roses, probably more than you might think. In my design, I have used a little under 40 rose heads.

*This large verdigris dish is a stunning feature in itself. Witness how it has been enhanced with a small mound of deep scarlet roses packed into its base. This is an excellent example of a successful marriage between two simple elements.*

# Golden sconce

The dramatic curves of this stately sconce made it a perfect item to embellish with flowers, fruit, and ribbon. I have given the whole display a sumptuous richness by spraying most of the floral material in glistening gold. The finished result is magnificent, with echoes of the baroque.

I have used the similar shapes of love-in-a-mist (*Nigella damascena*), safflower (*Carthamus tinctorius*), and poppy heads (*Papaver*) together with common wheat (*Triticum aestivum*), long-leaved eucalyptus (*Eucalyptus kruseana*), and rich, red roses.

Florist foam, tape, gold spray paint, and a rich brocade ribbon are the other elements needed.

Begin by taping a rectangular piece of foam upright to the back of the sconce.

Spray all the floral material, with the exception of the roses and foliage, gold. Leave to dry.

Next, wind your ribbon around the sconce and finish with a large rosette bow low down in the center. (To create this type of bow, see page 49.)

Take your largest poppy heads and place them in a group in the center, just above the rosette, to form the focal point.

Now work upward and outward with groups of love-in-a-mist and poppy heads grouped in threes and fives. Balance the arrangement, but it is not necessary to create symmetrical groups.

At the edges, add clusters of safflower and wheat.

For the lower edge, use longer stems of wheat and safflower.

For depth and interest, take a few stems of long-leaved eucalyptus and insert them around the outline.

Finally, add five deep red roses just above the center. This offsets the whole display and brings together all the other elements in perfect harmony.

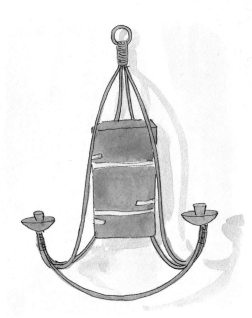

*For a sconce this shape, you need a rectangle of foam. Tape the foam to the sconce using masking or florists' tape. Other tapes do not stick so well.*

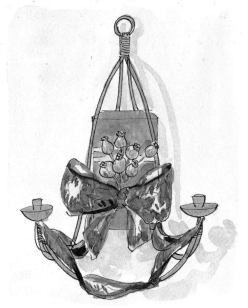

*Wind coordinating ribbon around the "branches" of the sconce and finish with a large rosette bow. Push in the largest poppy heads to form a focal point.*

A plain wall sconce is beautifully decorated with gold and red. Paint-sprayed wheat and poppy heads in glistening gold form the basis of the display; richly patterned ribbon hangs in luxurious drapes, while bright scarlet roses offset the entire arrangement. Dark green foliage provides a perfect backdrop.

# Autumn sheaves

Traditionally, grain was gathered into sheaves at harvesting. Their beautiful shapes and forms graced the church at thanksgiving services as people expressed gratitude for the crops gathered.

Today, these displays are once again admired for their simplicity and style.

WHEATSHEAF
A sheaf of gathered wheat is a perfect representation of nature's abundance and, because of its classical simplicity, can look stunning in almost any setting.

However, beware! When I first made a wheatsheaf, I thought it would be a very easy task to accomplish, but it can be deceptively difficult.

There is a recipe to success, although you still might encounter a few problems with your first attempt.

Take a bunch of common wheat (*Triticum aestivum*) and peel back the protective leaf which sheaths the husk.

Assemble string, a large newspaper, and sharp scissors. You will also need a natural ribbon, raffia, or grass to cover the string.

Place the sheet of newspaper, on a large work surface (I put mine on the floor). Prop up the sides of the newspaper with piles of books to form a cradle. Lay a piece of string across the paper, allowing each end of the string to drape over one side of the cradle.

Lay the wheat in the cradle, aligning the top of the wheat with the edge of the newspaper.

I used six bunches of wheat to fill my cradle.

Gather up the string and tie it loosely. Now, take your courage in both hands and, keeping the bunch exactly where it is, twist your wheatsheaf very slightly. (The second you pick up the sheaf, it goes everywhere, so do take care.)

*Traditional-style sheaves have become popular, yet their simplicity belies the skill required in their construction.*

Tighten the string, so that the sheaf can no longer move and trim the ends of the stalks flat.

Only now can you remove the sheaf from the newspaper and stand it up.

Cover the string with plaited raffia, a huge paper bow, or twisted grass tied in square knots, in the secure knowledge that the string underneath is holding the arrangement in place.

The sheaf would look equally effective using lavender or barley.

## HARVEST SHEAF

The vermillion colors of fall are collected together in this glowing sheaf. Orange, green, and gold jostle for position here.

I have used burnt orange safflower (*Carthamus tinctorius*) peeling out of their delicious green buds, golden ageratum (*Lonas*), and yellow, orange and salmon strawflowers (*Helichrysum bracteatum*). The whole sheaf nestles amid a feathery halo of black-eared barley (*Hordeum*).

You will also need on hand some natural and green raffia to tie the sheaf together. Although I achieved this arrangement by myself, it might be helpful to have a friendly pair of hands ready to assist in tying the sheaf together.

Trim all the stems so that they are the same height. Now take the safflowers, strawflowers, and some of the golden ageratum and gather them in a bunch. Try to intersperse the colors so that there are no clumps of the same hue.

It is important to keep the stems and flower heads level, so avoid putting the sheaf down until it is finished.

Hold the sheaf in one hand and with the other slip a loop of raffia around the stems. (Another pair of willing hands could help you here).

This is the tricky part, as you want to complete the sheaf with a circle of golden ageratum and finally a halo of barley for the outer edge.

The best way to achieve this is to keep holding the loosely-tied bunch and insert first the golden ageratum and then the barley until the sheaf is complete.

*Seen from above, the Harvest Sheaf displays its neat symmetrical lines and the halo of barley "whiskers." As this is all constructed in one hand, it demonstrates the need to keep turning the sheaf as you build it up. Different colors, for example pale pink, would create a more subtle variation on this theme.*

*Drape a large sheet of newspaper between two piles of books to form a cradle. Lay a piece of string across the newspaper, as shown, ready to take the wheat.*

*Hold the sheaf in one hand and loop a piece of raffia around it. Now add in the outer layers of lonas and barley. Do not put the sheaf down until it is tied.*

Now pull the raffia tightly. This action will pull the flowers into a dome shape and the stalks into a twist. Secure the sheaf with a tight knot.

To keep the sheaf in good shape, add another, thicker band of raffia, as this allows for less movement.

To finish, trim with wispy bows of green and natural raffia.

The completed display has the appearance of an impromptu bunch brought into the home from a country walk and certainly belies the patience of achieving this effect.

# MINIATURES, GIFTS, & ORNAMENTS

*In this chapter, I have explored various ways of using miniature arrangements to decorate objects in the home and other items more traditionally associated with a floral theme: hats and hair ornaments. There are also some clever gift ideas and ways of decorating wrapped presents with leaves or tiny floral posies.*

*Many of these ideas use small amounts of floral material, yet are just as effective as larger displays. Of all the designs in this book, the following ideas are sure to inspire you to adapt, experiment, and create your own novelties.*

# Miniature baskets

Charming little baskets have a special appeal. When selecting "ingredients," you will find you can use lots of reject material which is too short, too small or too delicate for other displays.

Look for little baskets in florists, department stores or even toy stores. They are inexpensive and can be transformed with a minimum of materials.

Each basket needs a snug filling of florist foam before you begin.

## WHEAT AND COBALT BLUE

Here, I have established an outline of common wheat (*Triticum aestivum*), filling in with the deep cobalt blue of the tops of delphinium. Tucked in are the complementary colors of poppy (*Papaver*) heads; they also add a delightful contrast of texture.

Choose some giftwrap ribbon of a complementary shade to tie around the basket and finish with a bow. Create the curls on the bow by pulling the blade of a pair of scissors along the ribbon ends.

## SUNSHINE-YELLOW BASKET

Cheerful little sunrays (*Enceliopsis nudicaulis*) nestle into this tiny basket. The stalks are very fragile, but on this scale you should be able to push them carefully into the foam. If some break off, simply glue them onto the foam. Once again, use a gift ribbon to complete the display.

## SHADES OF VERMILLION

The little oblong basket is filled with strawflowers (*Helichrysum bracteatum*) in shades of deep crimson and vermillion. I filled in with brown clubrush (*Scirpus*); you can use any tufted grass or reed here. Miniature poppy (*Papaver*) heads are tucked into this riot of color. The browns and beiges complement this rustic little basket perfectly.

## ROSE BUD BASKET

This mound of pale pink roses begins with an open bloom in the center of the basket and descends to the rim, finishing with tiny buds. Insert the roses close together to create a tightly packed display.

I wrapped pale pink double satin ribbon around the handle and underneath the basket before tying it at the side with a little bow.

## PEARL WHITE DISPLAY

The delicate form of bleached gypsophila or baby's breath creates the basis and outline of this elegant creamy-white display. A silver white everlasting or strawflower (*Helichrysum vestium*) forms the focal point; to add height and a shimmer of movement use bleached quaking or pearl grass (*Briza maxima*).

*Sunrays are extremely fragile when dried, but they are so pretty with their cheerful little flowerheads. Here, begin with a long stemmed flower in the center and work down the sides with two or three more flowers. As the heads are so large, you do not need many to make this display.*

*Several miniature baskets displayed together on a dresser or small bookshelf look most charming. Every one was quick and simple to construct and used leftover materials from other arrangements.* **Clockwise from top left**: *Wheat and cobalt blue, Sunshine yellow basket, Shades of vermillion, Rose bud basket, Pearl white display.*

## CHRISTMAS BASKETS

A lovely addition to the Christmas table, these little baskets are quick to assemble and make use of other decorations you may already have on hand.

The basket on the left is filled with varnished nuts, cones, and a gold-sprayed fir cone surrounded by stars on metal wire. I used shiny red "popper" beads individually as berries. The stars were bought as Christmas decorations, the beads were raided from my daughter's jewel box!

The larger golden basket is filled with poppy heads (*Papaver*), love-in-a-mist (*Nigella damascena*), and safflowers (*Carthamus tinctorius*).

You can buy these already sprayed gold, but it is just as simple to spray your own on large sheets of newspaper (although do make sure you do this in a well-ventilated room, or even outside).

The string of green stars was wound through the display.

To soften the whole effect, I used safflower leaves on the basket's rim.

*Shiny gold flowerheads and cones, glistening nuts, and Christmas balls and stars pack these little wicker baskets. Tiny baskets need only a few items to fill them.*

# Presents with a difference

To festoon gifts with ribbons and dried flora is easy and effective.

Gifts wrapped in textured papers simply beg to be trimmed with natural materials, and here are four pretty examples to charm and delight your friends.

### CHILI PEPPERS
Do not reserve these shiny seedpods just for cooking. Their crimson skins and twisting shapes make ideal decorations. White paper, which is embedded with strips of natural straw and fibers, is tied with a coffee and chili-red chiffon ribbon.

The chili peppers follow the contours of the bow.

### GOLDEN BROWN
Tan-colored paper is tied with patterned gauzy ribbon. The texture of the ribbon is picked out by the exquisite skeleton leaves. Orange Chinese lanterns bring out the warm colors.

### RAFFIA WRAP
Plait raffia or bind it thickly around a wrapped present. Tuck in bay leaves or wheat.

*Textured gift wrap lends itself perfectly to these natural trims. I have used wheat, raffia, chili peppers, bay leaves, Chinese lanterns, and leaf skeletons.*

There are really no rules here; use these ideas to inspire your own. Sometimes I have matched the flower to the ribbon or gift wrap; on others I have used a sharp contrast in both color and texture. This is also an excellent way of using up scraps of flowers or foliage.

### WHITE GIFT WITH FERN
Interesting white textured paper is decorated with white, gold, and dark blue striped ribbon. The dark pieces of fern form a striking silhouette. (Preserve the fern leaves by immersing them in a glycerin solution, see page 110.)

### BLUE AND GREEN PACKAGE
Colored raffia is a lovely parcel tie. Here, enriched green raffia binds stylish navy paper and finishes with a little plait.

### ORGANDY ON LACE
Deep blue and green translucent ribbon is decorated with pieces of deep blue delphinium. They are beautifully offset by the lacy background.

### THISTLES AND TARTAN
Extravagant carline thistles (*Carlina acaulis*) sit amid a shimmering plaid ribbon. White gift wrap is a perfect complement to the white background of the ribbon.

### COPPER BEECH
A multitude of harmonizing pink ribbons envelop this tiny scarlet package. Copper beech leaves are tucked into the riot of ribbons.

### LAVENDER BLUE
A glorious lavender dotted chiffon bow holds a small sheaf of lavender, both flowerheads and purple stalks. The textured white and mauve gift wrap forms the perfect background.

Transform a wrapped present into something really special by decorating it with swirling ribbon and a few little leaves or flowers. Scraps of fern, copper beech, lavender, and delphinium are used to good advantage here. Vary ribbon with natural or dyed raffia, either simply tied or plaited into ropes. Save a few lovely flowerheads for presents, too. Carline thistles combine perfectly with translucent plaid ribbon.

# Hair garlands

These delightful garlands are so easy to make and can transform the naughtiest minx into a forest nymph. There is an autumnal garland, perfect for fall or winter weddings, and a summer version. Obviously, you can adapt the flowers to suit your own occasion.

AUTUMN GLORY
For the fall garland, I assembled copper beech (*Fagus sylvatica*) and strawflowers (*Helichrysum bracteatum*) in rich burgundies and flame oranges. Wire, tape, and my glue gun were needed to secure the garland together, while a shimmering organdy bow in glowing complementary hues provided the finishing touch.

First, I crossed the base of two copper beech twigs together and secured them with wire. I brought them up and around my daughter's head and joined the more fragile twig tips together at the top with tape.

I left the leaves on the twigs and glued on a few additional ones where there were gaps, and to add a background for the strawflowers.

Next, I glued the strawflowers to the twig base, allowing them to "tumble" down the sides of the garland. Keep the heavier flowers at the sides and toward the base; use the lighter, delicate pieces toward the top. I left the top of the garland relatively free so as not to detract from Tiphaine's face.

Finally, I added the translucent ribbon tied in a luxurious bow.

*Pretty hair garlands in two seasonal variations can be made easily with materials you may already have. Most young girls would be thrilled to wear one for a wedding or special party.*

*Secure two beech twigs at the base with wire and bring them up around the head. Anchor the tips of the twigs with tape.*

## SUMMER CROWNING

My other daughter's flaxen hair becomes a haze of summer sun with this garland of sunshine yellow and white sunray flowers.

A thin wire coat hanger, natural raffia, and quaking or pearl grass (*Briza maxima*) are the other ingredients for this garland. Your glue gun and a little wire are needed to secure the elements together, and a translucent organdy ribbon adds the finishing touch.

I straightened out the wire coat hanger and circled it around Abigail's head. To match the other garland, I also crossed this one at the nape of the neck. Wind a

little tape around the wire to secure it.

I then covered the wire circlet by wrapping it with raffia and securing this with glue. I left the ends of the raffia to trail through my daughter's hair.

The sunrays are very delicate, so I used just the flowerheads, gluing them directly onto the raffia base, pressing them close together to create a chunky garland.

On the cross at the nape of the neck, I glued trailing quaking or pearl grass.

Finally, I tucked in the pretty organdy bow, and the summer garland was complete.

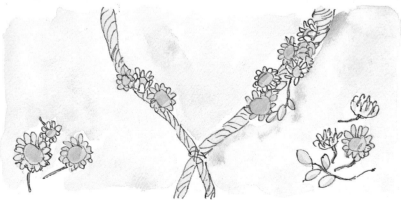

*Glue stems of quaking grass at the cross of the wire to give an attractive trailing effect at the nape of the neck.*

# Glistening nuts & cones

Baskets piled high and overflowing with lustrous nuts and cones make wonderful candle holders.

These arrangements are remarkably simple, relying only on your own eye to select contrasting and complementary textures and tones.

I used shiny filberts, chestnuts, and pecans against the rough texture of walnuts, brazil nuts, and almonds. A spray of varnish enhances this arrangement; do this before making your display.

One of my baskets already had holders for candles; for the other I squashed wire mesh into the basket and set the candle firmly into it. I then built up my arrangement, forming larger clusters of nuts at the base, securing them with the glue gun.

Try to arrange the clusters at varying angles for interest, and allow several nuts to "spill" over the edge of the basket to balance the weight of the display. Add in a variety of cones, such as pine and the smaller larch.

To add even more interesting texture, use beeswax candles.

*Based loosely upon the cornucopia, these laden baskets, burgeoning with nuts and cones, make ideal settings for candles, but also look good alone (**below**). Varnish the nuts for a gleaming effect; mix in cones to add texture and beeswax candles to provide a wonderful complement. Your glue gun is vital to create these overflowing displays.*

# Garlanded potpourri

Reflect the changing of the seasons with the aroma of potpourri. Here, two baskets are wreathed with flowers to represent the warm lusters of fall and the pastel hues of spring and summer. Essential oils to scent the baskets are easily purchased.

## SUMMER BASKET

The cream and peppermint green basket evokes a balmy, warm summer's day.

I selected a whole host of summer colors for this basket, and it is a good way of using up flowerheads or small items, as the materials are glued around the basket's rim.

Lavender, delphiniums, roses, wheat, *Nigella*, and strawflowers are the principal floral materials used here.

The basket rim is built up using small clusters of flowers (bound together with tape) or individual flowerheads. They are all securely attached to the basket with the aid of a glue gun.

Begin by gluing small clusters of wheat (*Triticum aestivum*) directly to the basket handle where it rises from the rim. Tuck in around this small clusters of pink roses, delphiniums, and the maturing heads of scabious (*Scabiosa stellata*), covering the previous stems and tape as you work.

Now work around the rim of the basket with clusters of love-in-a-mist (*Nigella damascena*) and the occasional clump of lavender and *Nigella orientalis*. Throughout this, scatter pretty pinkish pastel strawflower (*Helichrysum bracteatum*) heads.

Fill the basket with soft green love-in-a-mist heads, lavender flowers, rose petals, and any other pastel petals left over from other arrangements.

Scent the petals with a floral or rose oil for the perfect summer decoration.

*Summertime potpourri fills a specially decorated basket. Use fresh, pastel colors to achieve a summery effect, and any size basket – simply scale down the clusters of flowers decorating the rim. Use those flowers shown here to make your own potpourri, or buy a ready-mixed potpourri in summertime colors, topping it up with a few pale green or pink flowerheads.*

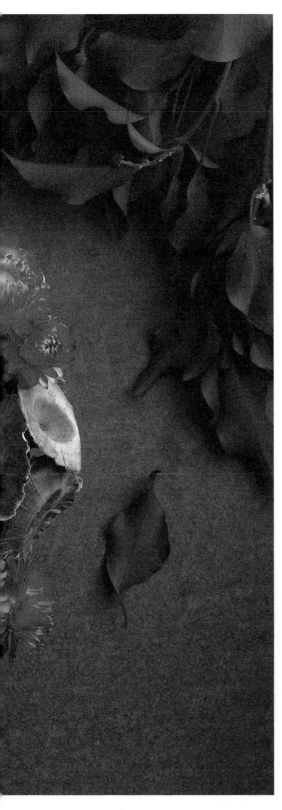

## WINTER BASKET

The warm, heady scents of dark winter nights fill this circular straw basket.

As with the summer basket, the rim is built up with small clumps of interesting materials. Here, I have used golden mushroom, deep flame-colored strawflowers (*Helichrysum bracteatum*), cones, and filberts. All the items are stuck to the basket using a glue gun.

Work around the rim a section at a time, gluing the items in small groups. Dotting pieces here and there does not work nearly so well.

It does not really matter what you put into the potpourri. Toning colors and interesting shapes work well, but do not forget fragrant herbs: basil, marjoram, meadowsweet, peppermint, rosemary, sage, and thyme in particular. Spices are also a good source of delicious aromas: aniseed, cardamom, cinnamon sticks, cloves, and vanilla pods are just a few that I use, as they are visually interesting, too.

Other wonderful winter scents include eucalyptus and lemon verbena, and finally do add twists of citrus peel for a sharp and contrasting essence.

*This basket demonstrates a great use for broken strawflower heads. You can buy these heads very cheaply if you do not have any. Mix with coffee-colored fungus and bobbly cones to adorn a simple, round basket. Fill with potpourri you have made yourself from fallen petals, aromatic spices, and flowerheads. Scent with a few drops of an autumnal essential oil such as orange. These oils are sold in health stores.*

# Clove and rose pomanders

There is little to compare to the natural, warm-smelling aroma of orange and cloves, or the deep, sensual scent of roses. Use these pomanders to decorate your linen drawers or closets and allow their delicious scents to permeate the fabrics within.

## CLOVE BALL

The clove pomanders are constructed on an orange. Use a thin-skinned "navel" type fruit or Seville orange; do not use a thick-skinned orange as it is very difficult to insert the cloves. Tangerines or mandarins are also unsuitable as they tend to be squashy and unstable.

Apart from the orange, you will need cloves, string, and plenty of patience!

Tie the orange with the string, dividing the fruit into four quarters. If you wish to use ribbon on this type of pomander, do not tie it on at this stage, as it can become stained by the juice. Instead, wait until the orange has dried, then remove the string and tie the ribbon in its place.

One at a time, insert the cloves into the orange in segment formation.

Now leave the orange to dry out. In doing so, it will shrink slightly.

Once the pomander is dry, you can begin to decorate the ties.

If you have used string or twine, you can add amusing details to the ends.

Here, I have drilled holes through nutmegs and slid these, like beads, onto the ends of the string. You could of course use wooden beads for a similar effect.

I have also glued bay leaves to the base of one of these pomanders to create an "elfin hat" pattern. Or glue on small cones.

Always look carefully at these small details, as they transform the mundane into something special.

## ROSE BUD POMANDER

The rose pomander is worked in the same way as the Clove Ball, except you use a dried foam sphere as your base.

Divide the sphere in half with a narrow satin ribbon and begin inserting the rose buds carefully into the foam. Finish with a bow for a feminine touch.

Perfect for the boudoir or your wardrobe.

Scent linen cupboards and closets with pretty pomanders made from delicious oranges and cloves or decorate your bedroom with tiny rosebud balls. Both types of pomander require a little patience to insert the individual materials, but the effects are long-lasting and make perfect gifts for friends or family.

Insert the cloves into the skin of the orange one at a time. Work from top to bottom in "segments."

Little details turn these pomanders into something special. Glue bay leaves at the base to create a little elfin "hat."

# Decorated hats

Fun and fanciful, a hat can adorn any plain outfit, transforming the ordinary into something memorable.

These hats are simple straw ones, economical to buy, and begging to be decorated. Here are three quick and easy ways to do this using natural raffia and a few dried flowers.

## NAVY STRAW
The simplest of all designs, this hat is also the quickest to make. Natural raffia looks particularly attractive against a black or dark background, and this navy straw hat makes a perfect setting.

Wrap lengths of natural raffia around the crown of the hat and bring both ends together in a long trailing braid, finishing with a knot.

Tuck a few merry little strawflowers (*Helichrysum bracteatum*) into the raffia band, placing a couple at the end of the braid. Make sure the flowerheads stay in place by anchoring them with glue.

## CHILD'S HAT WITH SAFFLOWERS
Begin by making a long braid from lengths of raffia. Secure the ends with tape and glue the braid around the base of the crown.

Next, make a full raffia bow and push a piece of wire through its center. This can then be twisted together and inserted into the braid at the back of the hat.

Do not attempt to make the braid and bow all in one, as the effect is too bulky on such a small hat.

However, for speed, you can buy natural raffia bows, already wired, to pop into a display. These make ideal hat trims.

For economy, and especially if you use a lot of raffia in displays, you might try to buy it in bulk, as it can be rather expensive.

*Brighten up plain straw hats with thick raffia bows or fat braided ropes scattered with delicate flowerheads or bold sunflowers. Grasses or leaves can add height and movement to the crown. These ideas are easily adapted with whatever material you may have left over.*

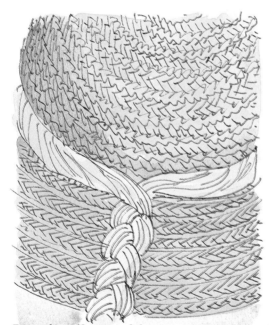

*Bring the raffia around the crown of the hat. Hold the trailing lengths quite tightly and divide them into three equal amounts. Now braid them together and finish with a neat knot.*

*Once you have secured the raffia braid and the bow, work in some pretty safflower heads. These are firm enough to push into the braid, but they will need a spot of glue first to secure them.*

**Left**: A chunky raffia bow is added separately to the thick braid around the crown. Safflowers are slotted into the braid close to the bow.
**Right**: Bold and brassy sunflower heads cluster on this simple hat. Grasses are used to add a little height to the crown and width to the floral grouping.

With the raffia trim complete, you are ready to add the dried flowers. I have used just a few.

Finally, take small heads of orange safflowers (*Carthamus tinctorius*) and insert them into the braid close to the bow. Secure them in position with dabs of glue.

### SUNFLOWER HAT
This wide-brimmed hat is a perfect foil for the huge exotic heads of the sunflower (*Helianthus annuus*).

Sunflowers have become more popular as dried flowers in recent years, and if you grow your own, it is well worth preserving them. The best method is placing them face up in silica gel. (For more details on preserving with silica gel, see page 108.)

Glue three or four sunflower heads into place on the brim and tuck in safflower (*Carthamus tinctorius*) foliage to add depth. If you prefer, you can wire the sunflower heads into the hat, although hot glue should be secure enough.

Instead of a ribbon, take curving black-eared barley (*Hordeum*) and fold it in half so that both ears and stalks can be visible. Bind the folded barley with tape and glue it to the hat. If you position these up against the crown, it gives a little height to the shallow crown of the hat.

Bunches of clubrush (*Scirpus*) or reedgrass (*Phragmites*) are also used in a similar way, fanning out across the brim and slightly up the crown.

# Creative candles

I adore candlelit dinners where you can shed the cares of the day and begin a relaxing evening. In the winter, I often have a candle or two alight in the room: the effect is most therapeutic.

Here, I have combined candles with flowers to bring a touch of luxury to your living room or the dinner table.

Do remember to take care when using lighted candles close to dried floral material. Most candle manufacturers recommend that the candle flame be always 2 inches away from anything which could easily ignite.

## WHEAT AND DELPHINIUM WREATH

Perfect for late summer evenings over the dessert and coffee, this wreath is built around an iron candle holder and a florist foam circlet.

I wanted this arrangement to appear to meander between the candles, but this can be quite difficult to achieve without having the whole thing look a mess.

To overcome this, I concentrated on using the main material: common wheat (*Triticum aestivum*), in clusters of threes and fives. Try to give each cluster a sense of movement, but be careful how you arrange the clusters in juxtaposition to each other.

As this candle holder allowed for the wreath to sit above the table, I was able to let several clusters of wheat point down. This gave the whole display a sense of fluidity.

In among the wheat, I inserted small clumps of cobalt blue delphinium. Make good use of these flowers by cutting the flowered part of the stem into sections; this gives you several pieces to cluster together.

For a final touch, push narrow green and gold ribbon in among the wheat to enhance the liquidity of this display.

## RUSTIC CANDLE HOLDERS

This is a clever way of using old cardboard tubes. Simply cut one down to about 3 inches and glue cinnamon sticks all around it. Tie it with natural raffia and insert a few bay leaves into this.

Alternatively, glue bay leaves onto the base of a candle and add a green raffia band at the bottom.

**Left**: *A stunning table centerpiece, this display of wheat and delphiniums is worked on a candelabrum. Weave some narrow ribbon through the display.* **Below**: *Bay leaves and cinnamon sticks give ordinary candles a rustic look.*

# Pretty packages

These two playful little containers are so effective, yet quite effortless to make. Tied with raffia as a present for family or friends, they are guaranteed to bring a smile of delight.

Look out for interesting shaped containers in gift and card stores, and remember that circular and rectangular shapes work well, too.

For the star, I inverted the box over a piece of florist foam, pushing the box down into the foam to make the shape, rather as you would when cutting out cookies.

Now tie raffia, string, or twisted grasses across the container to divide it into sections. Plant your areas accordingly. I have used cloves, cardamom, and pale blue statice (*Limonium sinuatum*).

The round woven basket is made in the same way, although you should be able to cut your foam to fit first, in the ordinary manner. I have planted this basket with statice, love-in-a-mist (*Nigella damascena*), and *Nigella orientalis*.

*Any shallow gift box or basket can be used.*
*Section the basket using raffia, twine or*
*colorful string. Tie an attractive knot on top.*

These charming little packages make attractive gifts for lovers of dried flower displays. Section small, shallow containers with raffia, twine, or thin rope and plant each section with flowers, spices, or seed heads. I have used the natural colors of cardamom, cloves, and Nigella, with bright lilac statice for a vivid contrast.

# Tools and equipment

Many people are daunted by the prospect of flower arranging, anticipating that it is necessary to have a large collection of specialist tools to be able to achieve professional results.

While not undermining the role of the florist, spectacular arrangements can be achieved with a minimum of materials and equipment.

Certain tools of the trade are useful, however. Some, you may already have, or can improvise. Others are worth investing in. Nothing in this hobby need cost a lot of money. And once you have acquired the basic tools, you will have them forever. Other mechanics, such as wire and mesh can be used over and over again once the arrangements are past their best. Even florist foam can be reused if the display is dismantled carefully.

With the correct materials, the art of dried-flower arranging is considerably easier to attain.

I have outlined those items that I consider are useful, but this list is by no means exhaustive.

**CUTTING**

For cutting stems, ribbon, and trimming off unwieldy pieces, it is worth acquiring large and small pairs of **scissors**, although a pair of good **garden scissors** will service most jobs.

**Dual-purpose kitchen scissors** with a notch in the blades for cutting wire are even better, as they save you buying separate **wire cutters**, which are necessary for cutting wire mesh.

A light pair of **clippers** are also useful. Keep a pair in your pocket just in case you see something interesting while out on a country walk.

I always try to prune carefully, even when confronted with the wildest abandon. It is courteous both to nature and the next person. (Do also pay attention to local conservation orders which prevent you from picking anything.)

When preserving with glycerin, a **sharp craft knife** or one with replacement blades will enable you to cut woody stems on the diagonal. This will help the plant to absorb the glycerin solution.

Florist foam is not difficult to cut, but a **long-bladed knife** such as an old carving knife will make this task even easier.

## WIRING

Most floristry books devote pages to wiring flowers, and in some cases, where the stem is too short or particularly fragile, it is necessary. However, my principal is to leave it alone unless the item is very heavy or unwieldy, as in the case of gourds, or if a flowerhead is extremely delicate.

You will find wire most useful when creating swags or wreaths, as it is a quick and easy way of making sure nothing falls off.

I use **medium gauge stub wire** for virtually everything, using two pieces together for especially heavy materials. The exception is quails' eggs. They are very fragile and need a lighter gauge.

Stub wire is sold in various lengths. It is more economical to buy the longest lengths that you can and then cut them down as you require.

Wire can also be bought on a spool.

Rose wire is usually silver and very fine; spool wire is thicker and quite often black. These types of wire are used to wrap clusters of stems together or to wrap a piece of stub wire to a single stem. However, I tend to cheat with clusters of stems, using tape to bind them together instead.

You can buy green florists' tape for binding a wired stem to disguise it. However, with the exception of traditional bouquets, it is not really necessary, as the wire disappears in the display. Alternatively, stub wire is available already coated green, should you feel any wire is likely to be visible.

Instructions for blowing and wiring eggs appear on page 114. For wiring materials such as pine cones and fragile flowerheads, see page 115. More details on wiring clusters of nuts or unusual items appear on pages 40–1.

## ADHESIVES

Extra strong all-purpose adhesive works well on many displays. However, it can be messy, leaving "snail's trails" of glue all over the flowers. Much better is a **glue gun** which shoots a spot of hot glue exactly where you want it.

The glue gun is wonderful and absolutely essential. It is extremely easy to use, does not smell, and the glue dries instantly.

A glue gun is relatively inexpensive to purchase and is readily available from hardware stores. I can say little more, except buy one!

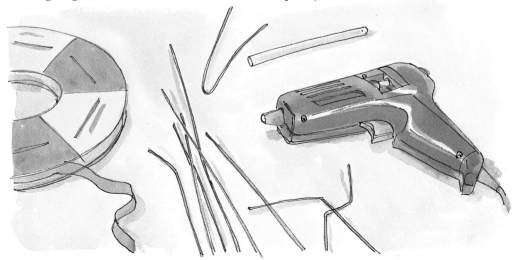

**TAPE**

**Masking tape** can be bought from art or home decorating shops, and is a useful alternative to cellophane tape. It is ideal for securing foam to an awkward base, such as a candelabrum.

Do not be ashamed of using ordinary **tape** for binding small bunches to be inserted into an arrangement. Items such as lavender particularly benefit from this treatment, as the less movement with these flowers, the better.

Green, stretchy florists' tape is only needed if you wish to disguise plain, wired stems.

**FLORIST FOAM**

Sold in bricks, blocks, cylinders, or spheres, make sure you buy the **dry-foam** specially prepared for dried flower arrangements. Dry foam is often gray or beige in color and appears more "dusty" than its wet counterpart, which has a spongy consistency and is usually green. Either can be cut to any size or shape using a knife.

Florist foam can be used more than once if it has not been stabbed by too many stems and is still intact.

**WIRE MESH**

Any arrangement which requires several pieces of foam together will benefit if held together with glue or florists' tape and then wrapped in **wire mesh**. The advantage of mesh is that it holds the foam together and helps prevent it from disintegrating. It also gives a much more secure base on which to wire heavy items like gourds or artichokes.

Fine chicken wire is also used in dried flower displays when forming a swag; although you can create a lighter-weight version with plaited raffia rope.

Chicken wire is most commonly sold in rolls in hardware stores or garden centers. Some florists sell wire mesh in smaller quantities, often "swag-sized" amounts, in packs.

A slightly more expensive plastic-coated version is available, which is kinder to your hands and to any furniture or fixtures it might rub up against.

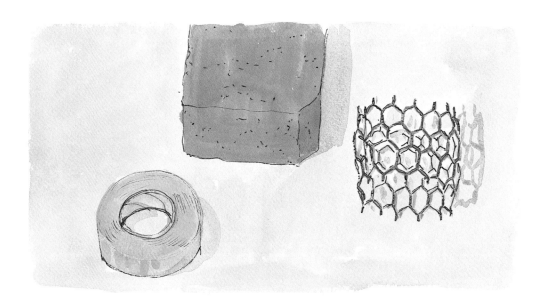

**Clear varnish** enhances the natural sheen of leaves and other materials such as nuts and is necessary if you want to use bread in a kitchen display. It is available in either a spray or a can. Spray varnish is probably most suitable for dried displays.

All sorts of interesting effects can be achieved using **car** or **furniture spray paint**. The natural straw hues of wheat and grass can be spray-painted to coordinate with your room or other elements of the display. Give lavender a richer color by spraying it a deep blue. This looks especially good in avant-garde arrangements. Alternatively, you can spray your container; cheap plastic containers can be transformed this way.

For more information on paint spraying, see page 114.

Specialist florist suppliers may also sell spray paints specifically designed for coloring floral foam; these are mostly pastel shades. However, you can paint foam with car or furniture spray paint.

**Metallic paint sprays** in gold, silver, bronze, and copper are perfect for use at festive occasions. Spray some of the items to be used: all foliage looks good (it will need to be preserved first with glycerin, see page 110). Poppy heads, *Nigella*, nuts, and cones are also particularly effective. Or spray the complete arrangement – container as well. Glitter can be sprinkled on before the paint dries.

Apart from spray paints, do not forget ordinary household paints. Water-based paints like latex are perfect for covering florist foam, or giving a plain terracotta pot a more interesting appearance. Latex or acrylic paints also dry quickly, too. However, they are not suitable for plant material.

To prevent some plant materials from disintegrating too quickly, use some firm-hold **hairspray**. It is perfect for lavender or fragile grasses which are prone to shed.

You can also buy commercial **plastic sprays**, especially for preserving dried flowers, from a well-stocked florist. **Artists' fixative** is another alternative.

## VARNISHES, PAINTS, AND FIXATIVES

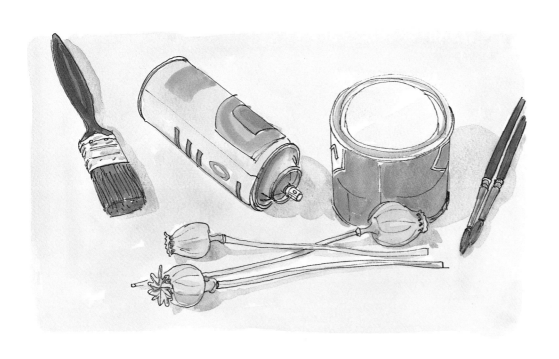

# Techniques

## DRYING FLOWERS NATURALLY

Dried flowers can be costly to buy, and it can add greatly to the pleasure of this hobby if you can dry your own specimens.

Do not think it is necessary to have a drying attic or barn where you can regulate ventilation, temperature, and humidity. I live in a small basement apartment with none of these facilities, yet I successfully dry many flowers.

If you are able to pick your own flowers, wait until the dew has evaporated, as it can cause brown spotting if left. Try to pick the flowers just before they are fully open and in the middle of the day when they have taken in a good amount of moisture.

Remove most of the lower and damaged leaves, then tie the plants in bunches; use a rubber band, as the stems shrink.

I make a feature of flowers that are drying, by suspending them from fine nails along my bookshelves. However, you can hang them in a cool cupboard, spare room, or other dry place.

The light in my apartment is dim which is advisable, as flowers dried in sunlight will quickly lose their color.

The length of drying time will depend on many factors: central heating, the density of the flower head, the climate, and the stage of the flower's development.

To test when your material is ready, the stems should be really dry; if used too early, the heads could drop and the stems could rot. Most varieties take between one to four weeks, although gourds need around three months; you will know they are ready if they sound hollow when tapped gently.

Grasses and reeds can be dried by simply lying them flat on paper. Spray very seedy grass with hairspray before trying to move them. This is also advisable for reeds, which have a tendency to explode. This happened when I left some in my car for a few days. The result was like a burst pillow, and I was picking the tiny pieces out of the floor mat for weeks!

Hydrangeas are best dried upright in a little shallow water. Artichokes and corn or maize are also best dried upright, but in foam or a jar.

Dry fungus in the heat of a low oven until firm.

If I am given fresh flowers, I always arrange them and, just before they begin to wilt, hang them upside down. Most survive, although some petals are shed.

It is always worth trying to dry any plant material; there is little to lose, and you could be pleasantly surprised by the results.

## DRYING WITH SILICA GEL

Silica gel is a drying agent which draws moisture from the plant. Although drying plants this way is time-consuming, the retention of the color and form is excellent, and the extra effort is quickly rewarded.

Silica gel is sold by drugstores; the blue crystals are by far the easiest to use. These begin blue and turn pink as they absorb moisture. They can be reused by drying them out in the oven until they have returned to their blue color.

Flowers preserved by this method should be in pristine condition. Ideally, they should be picked when they are completely dry, perhaps having been in the sunshine for several hours. The flowers should have also just opened, as this is when the bloom will be at its strongest.

Once picked, the flowers should be preserved immediately. If this is not possible, place the stems into warm water or well-soaked florist foam (the wet variety, not the sort used for dried arrangements). When you are ready to put the flowers into the silica gel crystals, cut off the wet stem ends.

Take an airtight container and cover the bottom with silica gel. Place the fresh flower on the crystals.

If the flower is a daisy shape, put it face down, lay delphiniums flat, and for other varieties plant the stalk down first.

Now build up the crystals tenderly around the flower and stem. Do not just pour the gel over the top as you will fracture the flower and the weight of the gel will tear off the petals.

Put the lid tightly on the box, taping it around the edges to make it really airtight. Plastic wrap are also useful for making a tight seal.

Now leave the box until the crystals have turned deep pink. For light, delicate flowers, this should take about 24 hours; for heavier blooms you will need to leave them for anything up to three days. Watch their progress by gently shaking back the crystals. The petals should feel like feathery tissue.

Double blooms and multipetaled roses are very successful as they seem to have more natural support.

This is just about the fastest way to preserve flowers and is certainly the simplest and quickest way to dry flowers in silica gel.

This method is excellent for fragile flowers, as the silica gel is not weighting the petals down for any length of time.

If you are only able to buy the large granules of silica gel and you wish to dry very fragile or fluted flowers, like freesias, which would be damaged by the larger granules, simply grind the silica gel into a powder using a coffee grinder or pestle and mortar.

Select your flowerheads and a non-metallic container which will sit happily in a microwave cooker.

I used long cardboard boxes which fitted in my microwave beautifully and also accommodated virtually every shape of flower I wanted to preserve.

As before, when using silica gel, the packing of the flowers is most important, so do take care. Do not heap the silica gel on top of the flowers, as the petals could easily distort or break.

Cover the bottom of the container with silica gel – either granules or powder. Lay the flowers gently in the gel either face up or face down, depending on the variety (see Drying with Silica Gel, opposite). Gently layer more silica gel over the plants.

Put the container into the microwave oven, uncovered. Next to the container, place half a cup of water.

Set the microwave to full power for 1–4 minutes depending on the type of flower. Delicate flowers take only 2 minutes (some even less); denser blooms will take 4 minutes.

When "cooked," leave the flowers in the silica gel for a while, until they are cool enough to handle. Then, as before, shake the gel gently to reveal the flowers beneath.

This is a most successful formula for preservation and I strongly recommend it, as the results are immediate and quite stunning.

## DRYING IN A MICROWAVE OVEN

## PRESERVING WITH GLYCERIN

This method is ideal for leaves which would otherwise crumble and flake. The glycerin replaces the water in the leaf, making it supple, glossy, and long-lasting. It does, however, change the color of the foliage, making it darker in shade.

Gather foliage for preservation well before the fall, as by then the leaf stops taking in water.

Mix one part glycerin to two parts very hot water. Once mixed, allow the water to cool before inserting the foliage, although woody stems can be placed in fairly hot water.

Remove all the damaged leaves and cut the stems at a sharp angle so they can absorb the glycerin solution easily. Very woody stems may even need hammering to guarantee good absorption.

Now stand the foliage in about 3 inches of the glycerin solution. Use a tall container so that the foliage is well supported.

How long you must leave the foliage will depend on the density of material. Gradually, the glycerin will replace the water in the plant and this can take up to four weeks. Check after about one week;

any glycerin "sweating" can be wiped off gently with a damp cloth.

If any leaves are withering, it is because they are not absorbing the glycerin solution. In this case, cut 2 inches off the base of the stems, hammer well, and replace the solution.

The process is complete when the leaves change color and feel silky to the touch.

Single leaves or small sprays can be totally submerged in a glycerin solution. This is considerably quicker, taking only about two days before the leaves are preserved.

As an alternative to glycerin, you can use car antifreeze, which contains ethylene glycol. This is cheaper if you are preserving large quantities of foliage; it also comes in blue, pink, and green, the colors of which transfer themselves to the leaves, giving the preserved foliage interesting tones. However, this mixture is poisonous and corrosive. Use plastic containers and wear plastic gloves. Do not allow the solution to come into contact with metal. Use the same ratio of antifreeze to water as described above.

# Plants to preserve yourself

Below and on the following pages are flowers and foliage most popularly used, and the best methods for preserving them. Obviously, some plants can be dried by several methods.

## DRYING NATURALLY BY AIR

Most flower varieties can be dried this way, and it is well worth experimenting. At the very worst, the flower will turn brown or the petals will fall off.

Very fleshy petals like freesias or narcissi are not always successful dried and need to be treated with silica gel.

Top-heavy items like globe artichokes and corn may benefit from having their heads supported on a wire rack.

Those plants without an asterisk can be hung upside down. Otherwise,

*     dry upright in shallow water
**    dry upright without water
***   dry flat

| | |
|---|---|
| Strawflowers | Barley |
| Roses | Wheat |
| Statice | Oats** |
| Lavender*** | Sunrays |
| Yarrow | Mimosa* |
| Dephinium* | Eucalyptus |
| Chinese lantern | Onion seedheads** |
| Hydrangea* | Goldenrod |
| Globe Artichokes | Bottlebrush |
| Corn/Maize | Blazing star** |
| Sea lavender | Broom |
| Gypsophila* | Chrysanthemum** |
| Teasel** | Zinnia* |
| Gourds*** | Peony |
| Love-in-a-Mist | Rosemary |
| Poppy | Sage |
| Moss*** | Bachelor's button |
| All grasses*** | Rush |

## DRYING IN SILICA GEL

This method preserves the color and form of the flower closer to its fresher state. It is more time-consuming, but the results are stunning.

You can speed this process up with the help of a microwave oven, of course. See page 109 for more details.

| | |
|---|---|
| Geranium | Marguerite |
| Bells of Ireland | Sunflower |
| Camellia | Violet |
| Marigold | Roses |
| Carnation | Peony |
| Fuchsia | Bachelor's button |
| Love-in-a-mist | Delphinium |
| Heather | Ranunculus |
| Lily | Freesia |
| Mimosa | Hellebore |
| Crocus | Zinnia |
| Daffodil | |

## PRESERVING IN GLYCERIN

This is a good method for virtually all foliage. Although it changes the color of the leaves, it makes them rich and glossy in appearance. They can also be wiped with a damp cloth, unlike other dried materials.

Chinese lanterns and gypsophila also benefit from being preserved with this method, as it prevents them from becoming brittle. However, it is not recommended for most flowers.

| | |
|---|---|
| Bay | Eucalyptus |
| Hawthorn | Hydrangea |
| Rowan | Ivy |
| Viburnum | Laurel |
| Rhododendron foliage | Magnolia |
| Willow | Oak |
| Barley | Wheat |
| Beech | Holly |
| Boxwood | Hops |
| Bracken | |

# Construction techniques

Many books devote pages to intricate techniques such as wiring. However, I am a great believer in avoiding difficult steps where possible and, instead, tackle many things by instinct.

So here are several of the elementary principles which I employed while working with dried flowers.

With these illustrations, I have provided a series of references to help you construct some of the projects in this book.

**Paint Spraying**

This is best done outdoors or in a well-ventilated room. Put the items to be sprayed on sheets of newspaper. Shake the can well and spray. When dry, turn the pieces over and spray again.

EGGS

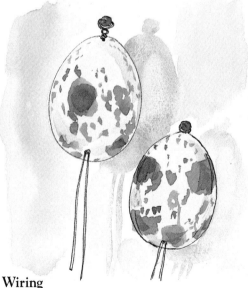

**Blowing**

Push a hat pin or large needle through the length of the egg. Then gently ease away a little shell from the blunt end by wiggling the needle. Blow at the pointed end and the contents will empty out.

**Wiring**

Thread 1¼ inches of 8-inch-long stub wire through a bead. Bring the wire back on itself and twist the two ends together right up to the bead. Now thread the beaded wire through the egg from the pointed end.

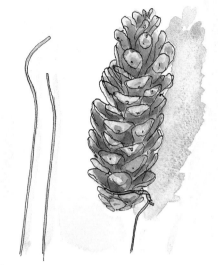

WIRING

### Cones

Push one end of the wire through the lowest band of scales and out the other side, leaving a little wire protruding. Push this wire back around the cone and twist the two ends of wire together.

### Fragile Flowers

When the stem and head is very delicate and you cannot use glue, it is worth wiring. Simply loop a piece of wire, place it close to the stem, as shown, and tape the end of the wire to the stem.

### Gourds

Any heavy items like corn or gourds need special attention. Bore two holes in the base with a skewer. Push a piece of heavy gauge stub wire through both holes and twist the ends together.

### Clusters

This is so simple. Just gather together a small group of flowers or foliage. Bind their stems together with tape; they are now ready to insert – as a whole – into the arrangement.

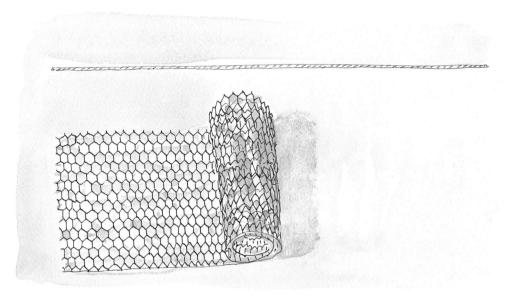

SWAGS

Determine the length and depth of your swag by using a piece of string. Drape the string along the table or shelf you are decorating. Remember that the swag will be full of ingredients when finished, so do allow for this. When you are satisfied with the position, cut the string and lay it down on a flat work surface. You are now ready to cut a piece of chicken wire to this length.

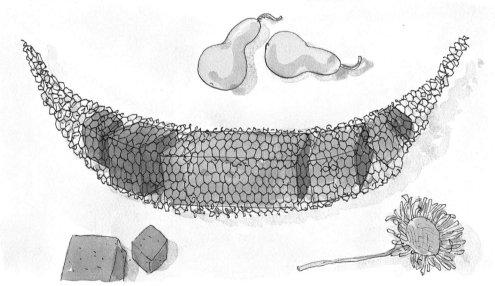

Once you have laid out the wire, place one brick of florist foam in the center. Take another brick of foam and cut it in two; place one piece on each side of the first brick. Now, mold the wire around the foam into a swag shape, bringing the ends up on each side. As you work, tuck in any sharp wire edges; they can easily scratch your hands or the furniture.

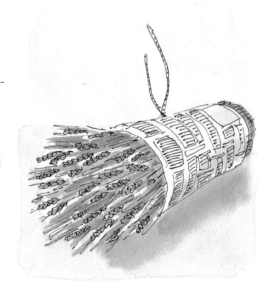

Line a pot with crumpled paper and a plastic bag. Half-fill the bag with plaster of Paris and insert the trunk. Top up the bag with more plaster and leave the tree to dry overnight.

To make the head, push the foam sphere onto the trunk to make an impression. Gouge out a little of the foam to make a hole. Glue the trunk into the hole, pushing the two firmly together.

**TOPIARY TREES**

To make a traditional wheat sheaf, you will need to lay a large newspaper between two piles of books. Lay a piece of string across the newspaper as shown. Now lay bunches of wheat in the newspaper.

Bring the sides of the newspaper up around the wheat and tie the string once around the bunch. Keeping the bunch where it is, twist it very slightly and tighten the string.

**WHEAT SHEAVES**

## TRANSPORTING AND STORING

Dried flowers do not like to travel, so where possible, assemble your display on location. If you do have to make it in advance, make sure that everything is well secured. Pack it in a large carton with plenty of space and swathe dark tissue around the arrangement.

Arm yourself with your glue gun, some wire, and hairspray for on-the-spot repairs.

For long-term storage, pack flowers in large boxes with layers of dark tissue paper gently supporting the heads. Put in a small pack of silica gel to absorb any atmospheric moisture.

## CLEANING

Dust, moisture, and direct sunlight are dried flowers' biggest enemies. Normal household conditions (although preferably not in a bathroom or kitchen if you want the arrangement to last for very long) are ideal.

A gentle flicking action with a feather duster can remove some dust, although "spiky" items like sea lavender or strawflowers do not always take kindly to this as they can get hooked up on dusters, even with the gentlest of actions. It is probably best to use a hairdryer on a minimum, cool setting to blow away the dust.

Depending on the flowers used, a realistic life expectancy is a year to eighteen months.

# Seasonal Flowers and Fruits

Gathering flowers in harmony with the environment and drying what you find becomes an absorbing hobby.

Wherever you live, there is always the possibility of collecting some materials. I live in central London with only patio tubs as my garden, yet I remain amazed at the wealth of things I find while cycling and walking around the city.

The variety of plant life in our natural environment is increasingly threatened so, while I encourage you to forage and be aware of all that is available to you, use common sense and consideration. Make sure you do not pick anything where you are not meant to (many local laws prohibit picking or removing plant material) and that you avoid trampling any other plant life. Always use a sharp pen knife or clippers, even when cutting grass, as you might needlessly pull up the whole clump.

## SPRING

Spring brings forth early flowers and budding twigs. On muddy walks in country lanes, look out for lichen-covered fallen branches, twisted vines against tree trunks, and occasionally – beneath holly and magnolia – skeleton leaves that nature has prepared for you.

In my London tubs, I have azaleas, rhododendrons, and camellias; and they all respond well to drying in the microwave oven with silica gel.

Bulbs are peeping through the solid earth and emerging into a multitude of colors. Although fragile, some of the delicate daffodils and narcissi can also be dried. They respond best to the microwave method.

## SUMMER

Summer's abundance brings so many flowers, it is difficult to choose what one might need. All the herbs are ripe for gathering during the summer months. If they are cut early, most herbs will produce again before the fall.

Look out for the many garden flowers; the wonderful colors and textures of the peonies and delphiniums, the scents of lavender and roses.

The extensive family of grass boasts more than two hundred species. Many of them can be dried. Also be aware of the hearty globe artichoke flower and – at the other end of the scale – the delicate gypsophila; both can be dried successfully.

As spraying is less frequent along roads, many elegant weeds are again available for picking. Cow parsley is charming when the seeds have formed; and look out for plants like burdock.

Gather prime leaves and twigs, as this is the best time to preserve them.

## FALL

Fall brings a harvest of fruits, berries, seed pods, and even fungi. Many flowers can be left to dry naturally on the stem. The hydrangea is a good example, as are most seed pods.

The thistles and heathers, wheat, corn, and barley, the fat gourds and sun-ripened maize: all dry beautifully.

Honesty and Chinese lanterns can be found rattling in the wind. And search for wooden beechnut casings.

## WINTER

Winter brings wind-fallen cones, seed pods rippling in the wind, and berried holly, ivy, and boxwood.

Take out of the cupboard cinnamon sticks, nutmeg, and star aniseed. Use orange, lemon, and lime peel for your potpourri.

At this time, I indulge in all the florists' flowers, like the forced hybrid roses which rarely open. When they look a little droopy, I hang them on my book shelf and prove that nothing need be wasted.

# Plant Directory

As a useful reference, I have listed here all the plants I have selected while preparing the displays for this book. I have listed them alphabetically both by their Latin names and those names by which they are most commonly known; sometimes the two are the same, for example, hydrangea! However, this list is primarily to help you if you wish to seek the same ingredient. Many times, I have seen something I like because of its shape or color. Only later have I had to find out what it is called, when someone asks me what it is!

| Common name | Latin name |
| --- | --- |
| Barley | Hordeum sp. |
| Beech foliage | Fagus sp. |
| Bun or grimmia moss | Grimmia pulvinata |
| Cape honey plant | Protea compacta |
| Carline or stemless thistle | Carlina acaulis |
| Chinese lantern | Physalis alkekengi |
| Clubrush | Scirpus sp. |
| Clubmoss | Selaginella sp. |
| Delphinium or candle larkspur | Delphinium sp. |
| English oak | Quercus robur |
| Eucalyptus leaves | Eucalyptus sp. |
| Everlasting or strawflower | Helichrysum sp. |
| Golden ageratum | Lonas sp. |
| Globe artichoke | Cynara scolymus |
| Guelder rose | Viburnum opulus |
| Gypsophila or Baby's breath | Gypsophila sp. |
| Hare's tail grass | Lagurus ovatus |
| Hydrangea | Hydrangea sp. |
| Lavender | Lavandula sp. |
| Leucodendron | Leucodendron plumosum |
| Love-in-a-mist | Nigella damascena |
| Peony | Paeonia lactiflora |
| Poppy seed heads | Papaver |
| Quaking grass | Briza maxima |
| Rattan palm | Calamus sp. |
| Reed | Phragmites sp. |
| Rose | Rosa sp. |
| Safflower | Carthamus tinctorius |
| Scabious or starflower or paper moon | Scabiosa stellata |
| Sea lavender | Limonium tataricum |
| Sneezewort or The Pearl | Achillea ptarmica |
| Soft rush | Juncus effusus |
| Starflower or scabious or paper moon | Scabiosa stellata |
| Statice | Limonium sinuatum |
| Strawflower or everlasting | Helichrysum sp. |
| Sunflower | Helianthus annuus |
| Sunray | Enceliopsis nudicaulis |
| Teasel | Dipsacus sativus |
| Wheat | Triticum aestivum |

| Latin name | Common name |
|---|---|
| *Achillea ptarmica* | Sneezewort or The Pearl |
| *Briza maxima* | Quaking grass |
| *Calamus sp.* | Rattan palm |
| *Carlina acaulis* | Carline or stemless thistle |
| *Carthamus tinctorius* | Safflower |
| *Cynara scolymus* | Globe artichoke |
| *Delphinium sp.* | Delphinium or candle larkspur |
| *Dipsacus sativus* | Teasel |
| *Enceliopsis nudicaulis* | Sunray |
| *Eucalyptus* | Eucalyptus |
| *Fagus sp.* | Beech |
| *Grimmia pulvinata* | Bun or grimmia moss |
| *Gypsophila sp.* | Gypsophila or Baby's breath |
| *Helianthus annuus* | Sunflower |
| *Helichrysum sp.* | Strawflower or everlasting |
| *Hordeum sp.* | Barley |
| *Hydrangea sp.* | Hydrangea |
| *Juncus effusus* | Soft rush |
| *Lagurus ovatus* | Hare's tail grass |
| *Lavandula sp.* | Lavender |
| *Leucodendron plumosum* | Leucodendron |
| *Limonium sinuatum* | Statice |
| *Limonium tataricum* | Sea lavender |
| *Lonas sp.* | Golden ageratum |
| *Nigella damascena* | Love-in-a-mist |
| *Paeonia lactiflora* | *Peony* |
| *Papaver sp.* | Poppy |
| *Quercus robur* | English oak |
| *Phragmites sp.* | Reed |
| *Rosa sp.* | Rose |
| *Scabiosa stellata* | Scabious or starflower or paper moon |
| *Triticum aestivum* | Wheat |

# Index